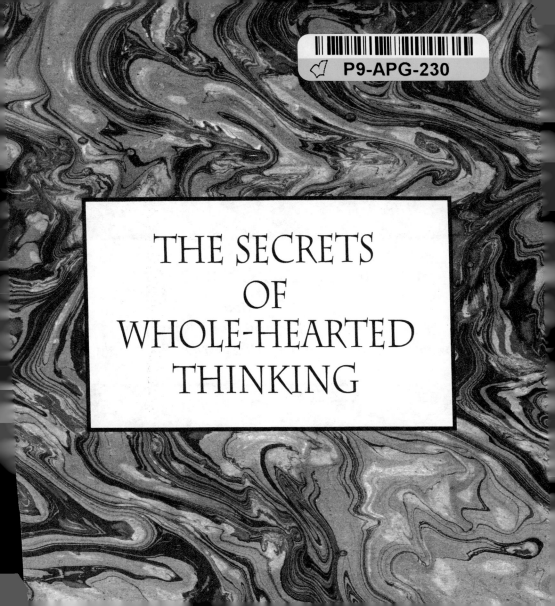

THE SECRETS
OF
WHOLE-HEARTED
THINKING

OTHER HEALING COMPANIONS

Good Grief Rituals
How to Forgive When You Don't Know How
How to Break the Vicious Circles in Your Relationships

A HEALING COMPANION

THE SECRETS
OF
WHOLE-HEARTED
THINKING

EVAN T. PRITCHARD

Station Hill Press

Published by Station Hill Press, Barrytown, New York, 12507.
Text and cover design by Susan Quasha, assisted by Anastasia McGhee.

Distributed by the Talman Company, 131 Spring Street, Suite 201E-N, New York, New York 10012.

Photograph of the author on page 132 by Richard Dentch.

Library of Congress Cataloging-in-Publication Data

Pritchard, Evan T., 1955–
    The secrets of whole-hearted thinking : 100 sayings, ideas, and paradoxes that can
    make your life fuller, happier, and less complicated / Evan T. Pritchard
       p. cm.
    ISBN 0-88268-160-5: $8.95
    1. Self-actualization (Psychology)—Quotations, maxims, etc.
    I. Title.
    BF637.S4P758 1993
    158—dc20   93-33283
                                                CIP

Manufactured in the United States of America.

Contents

Introduction

Included here are one hundred of the more memorable "epigrams" (terse, pointed statements, often paradoxical and presumably witty) from streetcorner advice, articles, and talks I've been asked to give over the years, sayings that seem to say "live a simple, balanced life—but live it whole-heartedly." I hope you enjoy them.

To feel whole-hearted, it helps to *think* whole-heartedly, using your whole brain, the intuitive and practical together. The secret to such holistic thinking is this: acknowledge opposites, then get them to work together for you. Try to see them as parts of a larger system. It's a practical approach because most problems are like a coin where we only see one side. It becomes valuable when we pick it up and look at both sides.

It's a shame so many people believe half-truths and end up living half-lives, feeling half-hearted. Live your whole life, and things will make more sense.

Complications happen when you try to change things without understanding the whole picture. Things become simpler when you take the time to see all sides of a problem. You might even find there is no problem. I call it eco-psychology, which makes it sound new, but it is actually very old—your great-grandpa probably knew about it and called it common sense.

The whole is made up of opposites that are really part of the same thing—thesis and antithesis, point and counterpoint, yin and yang. From this unity comes wonderful diversity, but put that perception of unity in words, and out comes paradox. The rational mind speaks in contrasts, while the intuitive mind speaks in simile and metaphor. But when they merge they often speak in paradox, for paradox is the language of balance. There are cold countries and hot countries, but the earth as a whole is lightly dark, coldly hot, vastly small, and now triumphantly in trouble, but we can't put it into words. We are having problems solving global problems such as ecology, because our experts are uncomfortable with paradox. We cling to black or white views, we choose this over that, meanwhile, our emotions are running rampant: the division we've created between heart and mind has brought us to the edge. We need to return to paradox in order to rediscover ourselves as whole people.

"Whole-hearted thinking" is a paradox in itself. Can the heart think? Of course, but only when the mind and heart become one.

Rediscovering the whole, inclusive human being that you are is not easy. It's a daily struggle, and we could all use help now and then. You don't have to be an addict to use a self-help book, you just have to want more out of life.

The success of *Life's Little Instruction Book* shows that readers are not completely bogged down in the complexities of today's world, and still willingly face the bigger questions in life: Why are we here? And more importantly, how can we get more satisfaction out of life while figuring out why we're here?

This collection is focused on making life simpler. If you wish to make life more complicated, or faster paced, if you want to amaze yourself with your own capacity for gamesmanship and intrigue, don't read this book. (Although I'm sure I could write a book about that as well, *this* one is only about simplicity).

Simply doesn't imply easily. Some of us have a long way to travel to get there—we are not all living on mountain tops or in aboriginal communities, and this book is not for those who are. It is for those who are trying to ride a bronco called America and want to keep their balance. It is for people who want to be simpler and more human, people who want to untangle life's problems and work towards re-integration of body, mind, and spirit.

Sometimes my answers know more than I do, and I enjoy it when that happens. When I've been asked to give talks or write articles—I'm usually the one who learns something. I've often thought that if I could collect all this "advice" and apply it to myself, I could live more whole-heartedly too.

I find myself using this book as a kind of "Human Being's Handbook," not some new philosophy, but a crib sheet on ideas that have always been around. I hope it expresses for you some of your own insights in a fresh, humorous way, suggesting through contrast, irony, and paradox, that the middle path is still the shortest distance between two points.

Evan Pritchard

THE WHOLE HEART

⁓1⁓

Relax, don't be lax.

You can have a whole heart as well as a clear mind. You can be peaceful yet productive. You can be spontaneous yet responsible. You can be simple yet smart. How? Relax and focus. "Relax and focus" may be the only mental "technique" you really need to know. It is a universal truth. It has been discovered by yogis, monks, baseball players, Olympic athletes, typists, eye therapists, writing teachers, musicians, mountain climbers, psychiatrists, and now by you. Experiment with it. It's one of the few things that all the world's religions agree on.

Focus, don't strain—relax, don't fall asleep.

People compulsively strain when they're trying to focus, either mentally or visually, and they tense all their muscles, including the heart muscles. No wonder there is so much anxiety in the world! The idea of relaxing any muscle in the body while focusing on something seems like a contradiction, but if you try it, you will see that it isn't. Focusing and relaxing are independent from one another, but when you put them together, amazing things happen. You can experience the satisfaction of living in the full spectrum of your human beingness when you don't have to close your heart to see clearly.

Here's an easy exercise you can try: Focus on an object in the room, while continually relaxing each part of the body. Then close the eyes, and keep focusing on the after-image. This is the poised mental state that can solve problems, recall facts and figures, or receive intuitive flashes. I've taught learning-disabled children how to memorize up to thirty-five random letters in this state. Many students fail because they try too hard, and in the wrong way. Don't respond to pressure with panic. Don't tense up, but don't blank out either. Find a balance.

Simple thinking doesn't have to be slow thinking. Mastering this one technique will enable you to be more successful in life, as you will get things done simply and efficiently without burning out.

❧2❧

First find your heart, then find your direction.

Find your direction, then find your circle. Find your circle and then find your sphere.

Since life is a never-ending road, there's no beginning. But every time you stop all thought and go within to find your heart, you're making a *new* beginning. You make each moment the first moment of creation whenever you dwell in the heart of love. Go back to the source as often as you remember to, and it will improve the aim of your life's arrow.

❧ 3 ❧

Do a heart check at all major crossroads.

Even if you don't feel the need at any other time, get in touch with your center when making a decision, or when a new opportunity arises. Most complexities can be traced back to an unsure or unwise decision. Decisions press upon us like weeds, and we have to be quick with the spade. There is never time to find out all the information, so the mind alone is not sufficient enough a guide for avoiding all complexities and sorrows and mistakes. Only the heart knows what lies beyond time.

In the old days, people would take time to gather in a circle and discuss each decision, put the facts together, and then when facts fell short, they would feel out the proper path in the softness of the heart, they would hear the voice of the guide in the silence and would see the light in the darkness. Today, we can do the same thing. If we are alone, we have the counsel of authors and books to discuss each decision with, as well as inner guides and ancestors. If we have friends, we discuss and ask for help. Then we go to the heart, for it knows what we can't.

Once the heart has spoken, "turn left, turn right," we must keep listening, for the road may turn again at any time. Once we have found our heart, we can find our direction, but not before. Until then, we may walk a straight and narrow path, but we are lost.

4

Once we've found our direction, we know who our friends are—we find our circle. If we grow our attachments first without any plan for our own lives, our mission in life takes a back seat to friendship, and friendship is shifting sand. A direction such as a career gives a point of reference and helps us see when and how friends are standing in the way of our progress. Again, the goal of the simple road is to find a balance between mission and family, but the mission comes first, and it has to come from the heart.

Once we've found our circle—people who love us, then we discover the sphere of our influence. If we don't find friends first, the sphere of our influence will be hollow with crowds of people who like us for the wrong reasons. If we have no circle, maybe it's not the time to put our ultimate plan into action. When we have the right friends, and the right direction, the circle will grow into a sphere of benevolent influence. It takes patience to approach success this way, but without patience, no success.

❧4❧

Feelings are facts,
but the facts are not changed by your feelings.

Feelings, emotional states, ups, downs, are what power us forward, they are our motivation for doing the right thing (or otherwise). Don't fall into the old trap of putting the word "just" before a feeling. There are people with feelings, and then there are robots, drones, and corpses. Feelings are power pep pills that give us strength and vigor and make our juices flow.

With feelings we can overcome obstacles, create miracles, heal others and ourselves, and learn the hard lessons. Without feelings we become abusive and controlling or become sitting ducks for abuse and control because we lose our individuality and self-determination, which is the same as what happens when we have too much feeling. It sounds simple, but the obvious answer is to live life with a moderate, on-going current of feeling running through. Avoid the mood swings, the highs and lows, avoid extremes.

Just as we can fast from food, and fast from negative thoughts, we can fast from emotions as well. Sometimes we can sustain a great deal of mental clarity and conserve energy by stopping the flow of emotions, and this is healthy and cleansing. However, it is dangerous to get trapped in that state. The health benefits of any type of fasting, be it mental, physical, or emotional, peak after a time, then go downhill.

Feelings are always a response to some fact, even if you don't have any idea what. Facts are not usually the result of your feelings but are merely effected by thought and feeling combined. Keep thought and feeling in balance.

6

Thought, Feeling, and Fact interact as a family interacts. Each has a unique role to play, each effects the other the way a father, mother, and child effect each other on a long trip in the car. Thought is in the driver's seat, but Feeling is really in charge. Fact does whatever it wants to regardless and often forces the car off to the side for reality checks.

5

*Talk about feelings, but don't expect others
to march on your heart's orders.*

If you want simplicity, don't confuse processes with goals. Know the difference between them and give equal respect to both.

When things are going well, focusing only on the goal is wisdom. When things are falling apart, focusing only on the goal is denial. If the car is running well, it's best I keep my eyes on the road rather than on the dials. But if I keep driving even though I know the oil is leaking out of the car, that's denial. I'm ignoring the process and fixating on the goal.

Dividing the two aspects of growth is a good way to keep them in balance. When you're working alone, work with your feelings and trust the results, but don't get sidetracked from your goal. When you're working with a group, have your meetings address both processes and goals as such, not all mixed together. Discuss your feelings in the context of everyone's right to discuss theirs. You have a right to say, but others have a right to disagree. The group process includes the group's feelings. Some people's cultural upbringing has given them more of an affinity for either process or goal, and they may try to compensate by going to the opposite extreme. You can respect their efforts to become balanced without falling in the same ditch with them. All roads lead to Rome, but they certainly don't all come from the same place!

❧6❧

Love is seeing yourself and your other as two people in the same boat—even if you'd like to sit at the opposite end of the "boat" sometimes.

Love is many things—the list goes on forever, as some writers have demonstrated. I will only say this: it's hard not to love someone in the same boat as you. Especially if they know how to row.

The interesting part comes when they can't row, or if *you* can't row and they *know* it. Then you have to talk to each other before drifting out to sea. Talking to someone you love is an amazing thing. Some will be amazed to find out what a small world it is, that two people could be so alike. Others will be amazed to find out how big the world is, how no one is just like you no matter how much you'd like them to be.

Have you ever stopped rowing long enough to think that everyone in your family is in the same boat? That everyone in your city is in the same boat? That everyone in your company is in the same boat? That everyone in the world is in the same boat? If you can fill that boat with love, you have the secret to whole-hearted thinking.

❧ 7 ❧

Don't do unto others as you would not have them do unto you.

No, this is not a double negative. If you really "do unto others as you would have them do unto you," you are imposing your values on others. When the Europeans came to America and converted the Natives, they were doing unto others...from their point of view. The results were tragic. Putting it in the inverse perspective "don't do unto others" is good preventative medicine, like "when in doubt, don't." Putting it into words is tricky, but so is *not* putting it into words.

～8～

Listen, listen, listen — To others, to spirit, to yourself.

Say this simple affirmation over and over every day, and then listen to what you're saying. You are opening up your awareness the most natural way there is, and there is no end to what you can learn. Listening is the lost secret of the ancients. The depth and patience of their listening was beyond our imagination. They weren't just "open" to spirit, they were on the edge of their seats.

Most of us jump to this depth of listening only in emergencies, disasters, or catastrophes. There are moments when every sound in the world is filled with meaning, every thought in our head has great significance, and every word from a friend is a gift from on high. Why do we abandon this state so quickly?

Sit still for a few minutes and let the noise clattering around in your head roll to a stop. Then listen to the sound of silence. Ask a question of the universe, not a trivial question either, but something worth knowing, something from the deepest shadows of your heart. Then go for a walk around the block, slowly, thoroughly. Walk on every pebble with thoughtfulness. Keep your mind free for any illuminations that might come to you, triggered by a bird, a cloud, a memory, a voice. This is the beginning of deeper listening, and there is no telling where it will lead.

✌9✌

Love people and even your blunders will be beautiful.

Harbor secret anger and your most generous efforts develop some strange twist.

Actions are commitment. Without commitment, there is no transformation. There are two kinds of actions: one is the action of the student—the explorer, seeking a vision, seeking blindly for the truth in the darkness; the other is the action of the teacher—the leader, wayshower, the vehicle, manifesting a vision from within.

We all have moments of both, so know the difference. Don't lead without vision, and don't hide in the darkness when you have something to say.

Either way, if you can only love, your explorations will be fruitful. Love will lead you into the light when you are without vision. Love will transform your confusion into wisdom.

If you choose to be of service to others, love will make even your mistakes fruitful (through some strange twist). Love will use you for healing even when you're sick. Love will lead and serve through you and even your blunders will be beautiful.

A BALANCE IN ALL THINGS

❧10❧

If at first you don't succeed, try two hands clapping.

You probably know the old Zen koan, "What is the sound of one hand clapping?" I think the Roshi who coined that phrase was trying to find a polite way to say "Silence!!" to an over-talkative student, but it still makes an important point. The one hand is the still point of meditation where all is one—silent and unchanging. If there is only one hand, so to speak, how could there be sound?

The key to whole-hearted thinking is this: When you see beyond duality, there are no longer two sides to the coin, just one coin. But you need to have seen both sides first.

People see one side of a coin and say "it's all one coin, so why pick it up?" and assume the hidden side is the same as the unhidden side. They use one side of the brain, one philosophy, one extremist view, and think they've achieved nonduality because life is so monotonous. It's not even practical. It's like jumping around on one foot all the time. God has two feet, and they're in your shoes. Go out and explore.

If you can't fix the whole engine, break it down into parts—but make sure you put it back together. If you can't fix your life, look at the parts, learn about balancing, refueling, positive and negative charges, cause and effect, momentum and gravity, but remember to put it back together. Then when you really see how all life interconnects as one, then answer the question, "what is the sound of one hand clapping?" A lot like the sound of one world spinning, I suppose.

Understand duality and then find the center. The one who has made the journey from one-sidedness, to two-sidedness, to no-sidedness can balance life's opposites and get the work done "with both barrels blazing" without leaving the calm center.

৵11৵

Diversity doesn't destroy unity, it's an expression of unity.

There is only one way the universe could work, and that is in unity expressed in diversity. This principle is fundamental to the duration of the universe, and if you don't believe me, ask God.

The old expression, "It takes all kinds to make a world," which probably dates back to Noah's Ark, is truer than we know. Each piece of creation is unique. The Creator follows Picasso's example and never crosses the same artistic river twice. Life arranges and rearranges basic building blocks of vital forces into ever-new varieties of creation, no two alike. Snowflakes are fractal constructions based on very few possibilities, random patterns within strict parameters. And yet no two have ever been exactly alike, although if you've ever been to Maine in the winter and seen all that snow, you'll find it as hard to believe as I do.

If life is controlled chaos and is not controlled by us, then trying to control everything is a dumb approach to life and only leads to confusion. Setting up hierarchies where the person at the top is responsible for the actions of every underling only makes sense if it's one based on understanding and guidance rather than control. Police states create incredible complexities underneath the surface, as life finds clever ways of meeting its needs.

ᴄ12ᴄ

From variety arises strength, from complexity comes confusion.

The difference between variety and complexity is understanding. When life is humming like a beehive, there is abundance and variety. When things go wrong, people get together and work out solutions. When people get anxious (or arrogant) and don't take time to understand the system, or grasp the problem, things get fixed wrong. When things are fixed wrong, then complexities multiply. When complexities multiply, things break down and can't be fixed, and then the variety starts to disappear. When a system reaches this kind of complexity, people get confused. When people get confused, instead of seeing the wonderful diversity of life's cornucopia, they see only complexity, and start to cut themselves off from the whole—the history of New York City in a nutshell.

People who seek the wrong solutions to their health problems find the problems get more and more complicated, just like urban centers. When society breaks down, the problems reach a breaking point and everyone leaves or there is a revolution, and it starts all over. When a person's health breaks down, they get sick, die, and have to reincarnate and better luck next time. Don't let this be you. Compensate for past imbalances, and then seek the middle path gradually. If you ate too much meat, eat vegetables. If you pushed too hard, rest. If you thought to much, try exercise. If you indulged too much, fast. If you were too passive, be more assertive. If you ate too little, eat more. Then move slowly toward the middle.

❧ 13 ❧

Enlightenment often comes after struggling with the problem and giving up.

Release comes in a moment of balance between being aggressive and passive, between willfulness and surrender, between effort and effortlessness.

You've probably noticed that some inner goals are only achieved after a long, protracted struggle. You worked at it without results, you gave up, you forgot about it, and then it came upon you unawares. But why?

I call it the power of positive giving up. My motto is, "When in doubt, give up." But *how* you give up is important.

You can't expect to give up in an angry way, destroying everything you've been working with, and you can't just pretend to give up either, like you were bluffing the universe at poker. You have to do all you sincerely can do on your own, and then release it, give it up to spirit, as they say. Just forget about it.

Why does this work so well? It has to do with reverse effort. The handle to the door of life is on the *other* side of the door. (It opens only from that side.) You can't just throw yourself against the door and expect it to open. When the people on the other side hear you bumping and crashing, they'll open it, but not while your weight is against it. You have to step back and give it room.

Have you ever had someone ask you a question over and over again, never listening to your answer? Working the night shift in Heaven must like that, with all the praying some people do.

There are several stages to reaching any inner spiritual goal. First you have to build up a lot of energy around the issue. To do this, engage your emotions and desires and push that energy from deep inside you. It might even take the form of anger and frustration, but it doesn't have to. It can be pure desire in the positive, up-building sense. During this push period, you rarely get results, but you do get your mind totally focused on one thing. Ideas come, sometimes in fragments, sometimes whole.

The second stage is giving up totally, until you become totally detached from the results of your actions, totally relaxed.

As you swing from total involvement to total detachment, you hit a perfect balance point in between, if only for a second, and this is the window of infinite opportunity. This is the third stage, realizing your goal. This is where the chemistry is just right for miracles, the balance of desirelessness and desire, when you can relax, not be lax. If you can hover in this perfect balance for a while, it is incredible what you can do and become. But you need to have a good deal of energy invested, and that usually comes through hard work.

❧14❧

Notice opposites, then look for the unity in those opposites.

Opposites don't necessarily mean opposition. Opposites mean harmony, balance, and relationship, too. There is a counterpoint of atoms that holds the world up underneath us, and it's a counterpoint of opposites, positive and negative.

Opposites are fascinating. Everything in nature can be explained by polarity and this helps us to understand ourselves. Pure oneness is just as real and true and beautiful, but since you can't describe it in words and can't break it down into thoughts, it can be a dull subject of conversation. We can appreciate it best by studying the diversity and seeing the oneness beyond and inside it. But explaining oneness is like explaining a good joke—either you get it or you don't. The one you can talk about is not the one.

❧15❧

Don't change the world, change the person looking at it.

Don't change the world from the outside, change it from the inside. Don't change people's minds for them, change their hearts and their minds will follow. Teach, inform, share, inspire, but don't change, don't even persuade. No one has enough wisdom to persuade the entire world correctly. Consciousness is your most important possession, so give it away, but don't let others steal it from you. Consciousness is the house of the soul. Break and enter that house and you are trespassing. If you knock and someone says, "Come in," enter carefully because you never know what's in that house.

If someone says, "Don't come in," it's time to leave respectfully. That person is responsible for their own safety. If no one is home, you can't take over the house for some good cause, even if the hatch is flapping in the breeze. When they've ready, they will be glad far your help.

We are here to learn, not to sit idly under the trees. We are here to expand our consciousness because of consciousness. Without respect for consciousness, you don't understand anything, and only a fool would change what he doesn't understand.

If you want to change the world, be like yeast and grow in your own way and let it spill over into the hearts of those around you like wine. But first be leavened. If you want to change the world, be like a candle, and offer to kindle the fire of others. But first, burn brightly yourself. If you want to change the world, be like a songbird whose music sets off the whole orchard into song. But first feel like singing.

Changing the world is a questionable business—it's amazing how wonderful it already is.

～16～

Don't be afraid to ask others for help, but don't let them take over.

There is one gatekeeper in our head who wants to let everyone inside, and another gatekeeper who wants to keep everyone out. The first is the passive, the second, the aggressive elements within us. The first says, "How nice of you to come." The other says, "Who the hell are you?"

Generally, these two can get along because they need each other, like husband and wife. The first one is needed to lift the latch and open the gate because the second one can't find the release lever. Since some people are always going to try to take over and ruin your life once they're in, you have to have the "bouncer," the second gatekeeper, for survival's sake.

In more scientific terms, the first gatekeeper represents the subconscious receptors and communication systems that link us with the rest of this wonderful planet, and the marvelous human race, in particular. The second gatekeeper is the subconscious defense mechanisms and censors we have built in that help us survive on this miserable outpost on the edge of space and help ward off those insidious creatures, human beings.

In good times, these two make a great team. But, during a crisis, they can get into a shouting match. A person comes to the gate of the mind, and the first one says, "Please come quickly, we need help!" and grabs their arm, while the other one says, "Off limits! Disaster area! No one allowed in!" and starts shoving in the opposite direction. It can be pretty confusing for the innocent passerby.

For this reason, when things get out of balance, one may want to see a therapist, regardless of how much spiritual training your ego tells you you have. There can be an internal conflict where there is no easy solution. A healthy subconscious can ask for help without letting others take over, but a damaged one cannot and will either allow both or neither. The spiritual self or soul doesn't injure and knows who can be let in and who can't, but in order to hear the message during healing, we may have to separate the soul from the human self. But don't get stuck there like some religious fanatics have. Heal the damage to the subconscious through therapy. Then try interacting with others. If therapy works, we won't be afraid to ask others for help but won't let others take over either.

❧ 17 ❧

There are two wisdoms: the wisdom of planning ahead, and the wisdom of not planning ahead. Live wisely.

There is the wisdom of men, and that of animals. There is the wisdom of sport, and the wisdom of play. There is the Cosmos wisdom of the adept and the Chaos wisdom of the fool. One builds defenses against the darkness, but the other is open to a surprise attack from the arms of a loving universe. Both are wise.

There are two kinds of wisdom, but only one kind of sage. The wise man has room in his life for both empire-making and mistake-making. Empire-making lets a man test the strength of what is in his heart, though it closes the world around him. Mistake-making, on the other hand, if properly practiced, opens his world up to possibilities, while showing him the depth of his weakness. It makes his heart grow, even when the world seems to shrink. (The same applies to wise women.)

The secret is only to make new mistakes, never old ones. Never fall headlong into the same river twice, but once can be delightful on a hot day. If work is going according to plan, that's good: If life is going according to plan, you're not trying.

The wisdom of thinking ahead is a half-truth, but so is the wisdom of not thinking ahead. You can't live either way except half-heartedly. Accept both and you have wholeness and whole-heartedness.

How do you live the spontaneous existence of a Hermes, or Puck, and at the same time be the captain of your ship of state, or be at least someone you would want as a roommate?

Have you ever danced well, sung well, painted well, hiked, boated, or written well? Of course you have. That was *it*. Any means of expression done skillfully, whether at the office or the concert hall, insists on integrating two wisdoms, that of control and that of release, that of the fight and the soft surrender, the sure thing and the foolish risk. There is wisdom in wariness, because "other" people are so small, and there is equal wisdom in trust, because we ourselves are so big we can survive almost any pettiness. So trust...warily.

❧18❧

Make self-discovery the goal behind each of your endeavors, and no time is wasted.

Although the self is one, I have found that there are two poles, two directions to self-discovery. One is the quest for the spiritual self, the other is the quest for the objective self. Neither has a beginning or end, so I call them directions.

In many Native American cultures, the quest for the spiritual self is called the seventh direction. The spiritual self is discovered by tearing off the veils of complexity, peeling the layers of the onion away, until you reach the spiritual essence, the spark of life. At first, the part of the self that is purely spiritual may seem a small and puzzling part of the whole, but if you go off in search of the mystery as to "what is the Soul," you will find it is both infinitely large and infinitely simple. By making your life infinitely simple, you prepare yourself for an encounter with the spiritual. Know Thy Self.

Equally important in becoming a co-creator with the universe is to know yourself in the objective sense, as an anthropologist would know you. Know who your people are, how your personality was formed, why you like certain foods, why you like or don't like large crowds. What does it mean to be a male or female in your subculture? In Native Culture, these questions relate more to the first four directions; there is a race, a color, and a way of life that comes from the south, one that comes from the west, the north, and the east.

The objective self is discovered the way you might put a very hard puzzle together. First you might find a piece that interests you and seems to be a causal point of your personality. Then as you find pieces that lock into it, connect them until a picture emerges. You might find yourself saying "I know the puzzle has to be of limited size, because the box is only so large." Yet as you add one piece to another, none of them alike, you begin to realize how complicated you are, almost infinitely complicated. No wonder life's so confusing! Going back into the history of your family, you might find that many races were involved, and many historic events had an effect on your ancestors, and on you. Eventually you might conclude that if you went back far enough, you'd find you are connected to every race of man, and every other human being by blood. That realization, that all people are your certified brothers and sisters, is worth the trouble you went through to Know Thy Self.

Every situation you encounter in life can help you in your quest for one or the other of the mysteries of the self, and sometimes both. The one who is seeking this large a self will never run out of things to do and will never be bored. And no endeavor, no matter how disastrous it seems, will ever have been for nothing.

❧19❧

A balance in all things. Walk straight behind the plow.

Extremes are not stable. At the outer limits are dead ends. One always learns from breaking through limits, but one needs to eventually come back to the middle ground. Even an eagle lands once in a while.

By playfully combining opposites, we keep moving forward, keeping our balance. Plow your field, but don't get in a rut. When we are children, we dance on the fields and leave only a few footprints, so it doesn't matter where we dance, as long as we don't step on the flowers. But when we are adults, especially if we are parents, we are pushing a plow much of the time, and it *does* matter where we walk. We have a responsibility to the future—every step leaves a long-lasting mark in the soil. We must take care that the blade doesn't do damage, and that we plant good seeds. Otherwise, we remain as dependents and never become sovereign.

The balanced person spends time giving to others, and time working on themselves, time being a channel for the spiritual, and time cleaning the pipe. We are part selfish and part unselfish. Each of us carries a sack of pearls over one shoulder, and a sack of poop over the other. Whether we are ship masters or galley slaves, we have these two sacks. There is no one living who is also perfect, and no one living is without a gift, or at least a door prize from the universe.

Because we live in a world of such opposites, we need to be careful where we walk, the person ahead of us might have had a hole in their bag, just as we might have holes in our own. So walk each road with care, as if it were covered with treasures, and also as if it were covered with poop. Balance is the secret to success in such a mixed bag as this world is.

27

SLOWING DOWN
(THE TURTLE TEACHINGS)

❧ 20 ❧

The slower you go, the faster you grow.

I learned this expression from a music teacher who had an amazing ability to learn new music in record time. (He could also play very fast.) He taught me that if I started out very slowly and learned it right the first time, I could progress quickly. I share this with my own music students, although I notice that many of them still try to master music as if they were running hurdles and burn out quickly.

I also learned the same teaching from a Native American Medicine Man whom I call Grandfather Turtle. Once, he was giving advice to a woman whose life was confused and complicated. As she spoke of her problems, a turtle walked up to them. He pointed to the turtle and said, "See how that turtle is walking? He goes real slow, and takes one step at a time, but he never makes a mistake. He takes a step, then looks around, then takes another step when he's all ready. Turtles have been around a long time, and they're very wise. Listen to that turtle. If you stop rushing around, maybe spirit would catch up to you." (She didn't slow down, and got a speeding ticket later that afternoon, so I heard.)

❧21❧

Start slow, and let the pace catch up with you.

There is a lot to be learned by doing clerical office work. If you start slowly and calmly and memorize the movements of a new task, you can speed up gradually. Soon you have made up whatever minutes you lost going slow. Like practicing scales, routines can be fun if you can do them quickly and well, and that comes from proper preparation. This approach is one of the best ways to reduce stress and anxiety without falling behind in your work.

Now that most automobiles have automatic transmission, we've forgotten the principle of starting in first gear, but standard shift (the traditional way) is much more fuel efficient. I find that I type slower in the morning and get faster and faster toward midday, and so I don't fight that. At worst, it all comes out the same by the end of the day.

I also believe in starting small. To agricultural people, starting small is obvious. Seeds are small, nuts are small, baby farm animals are small. You protect them and nurture them, and they grow large enough to support you. Even you started small when you were born, but for some reason, businesses today try to start out with a big splash and often go bankrupt.

Some corporations work as if they were running a race every minute. Good Olympic runners take care to start slow, and build up their speed over several days before a race. No good coach lets his runner enter a race cold, because the art of running is 90% preparation. The starting gun goes off near the end of a runner's job, not the beginning.

❧22❧

Get a rhythm going and others will join in.

Get your ducks in a row and others will line up to work with you. Magnets attract metal because their molecules are all lined up in a rhythmical way inside, and the metal pieces all want to join in. It's the same with people. Get in harmony with life and sing your song and people in agreement with you will be attracted to you.

Part of what makes music different from noise is its regular pulses, which can be found on many levels. A musical tone is a regular pulse. A time signature represents a regular pulse. Harmonic resonance is generally triggered by regular beats, or "periodicity." The whole universe works in modes of periodicity, and so the universe is musical, and resonance is everywhere. Resonance is why the whole is greater than the sum of its parts.

ᴥ 23 ᴥ

Tune the instrument before you play. Don't start off on the wrong foot. Wait until preparations are complete.

Another music teacher I studied with performed frequently on television, and on record. He taught that if you weren't in tune, it didn't matter how good you were. He refused to speak to you until your instrument was perfectly tuned. Most of us wasted our first lesson with him settling for a rough approximation, wondering why he wouldn't teach us. Today, I teach my students how to tune in three stages: economy, regular, and high test. If you approach each stage patiently, it doesn't take that long.

Much stress in life is caused by jumping in with elbows flying and fighting your way through a job you know nothing about to the end. Some employers encourage this, calling it "aggressive problem solving." Ask yourself if it would be possible to spend your own "organization" time studying the problem first, making the time up later by getting the job done efficiently. Native Americans tell us that if the European visitors had taken more time to understand what was going on here, we wouldn't have all the environmental and political problems we see today.

ℰ24ℰ

*Better to let others wait a minute
than to waste an hour doing something half-heartedly.*

If you give talks or perform music, you'll know what I mean by this. Construction contractors find the same to be true. Being exactly on time is a priority, but not always the highest one. The important thing is to have all the right materials for the job and the right mental/physical state. If you do have to delay an event to do it right, work backwards from there, *so that next time you think ahead and show up early*. There is truth to the expression, "The secret to success is showing up!"

✍25✍

The fastest way to speed up your progress is to slow down.

If your life is flowing along smoothly and you never have to backtrack, don't follow this advice. But if you are making mistakes, the vision of your purpose is blurry, or seem to be out of synch with your environment, take a few minutes to calm down and back up deliberately and make sure you're building your tower on your own foundation, and not the one next door. Slowing down seems to be the basis of eco-psychology and will lead to a saner inner environment. If every time you slow down you fall asleep, maybe you have a health problem or are over-tired. Slowing down may or may not mean lowering your expectations, depending on what they are. Most results can be achieved more intelligently and efficiently by starting slower.

Here's an example of spiritual math: If you have a half-hour to do an hour's work, contemplate for ten minutes. A whole drama can unfold in a dream in only a few moments of "real" time, because dreamtime is so concentrated. In that kind of "dreamtime," problems can be worked out as swiftly as a thought. A message can be delivered in a flash of lightning, a change of consciousness can happen in a moment. Ten minutes of real contemplation can connect you with dreamtime, and sometimes the first nine minutes don't count. It takes nine long minutes to slow up and slow down until you dip into the accelerated swiftness of dreamtime. It's that one minute beyond normal time that shows you how to accomplish an hour's work in the remaining twenty minutes. That's spiritual math and the secret to solving many of life's problems. To the problem-solving ego it may seem like cheating, but it's not; it is actually a power tool.

❧26❧

Don't rush ahead of your vision.
You might find yourself out on a limb.

Everyone who asks can receive answers from within, but some people hear the first part of the message and get all enthused, rushing out, never hearing the second part of the message. They rush ahead of their range of vision.

When they end up hanging from a cliff, they say to God, "When are you going to learn to give better directions?" The Almighty answers, "When you learn to listen."

The management takes no responsibility for customer's actions on hotel property.

❧27❧

If you ain't inspired to do it, ain't required to do it, ain't desired to do it, don't DO it!

The ambitious person works and works without questioning why the creation, and eventually becomes the effect of their own creation. The passive person finds many reasons not to be creative—thinking is risky business—and becomes the effect of others. But the wise (wo)man finds a balance in all this and holds valiantly to the middle of the road.

Complications come from compulsive planting. Simplicity comes from weeding out early. Before rushing into a new activity, ask yourself, "Am I really inspired to do this?" If you are inspired, do it while it's hot. Sometimes how you do it is all that matters, and inspiration determines how it's done. Even if you don't change history, good ideas will come, and you can use them in your next novel.

Second, if you aren't so inspired, ask yourself, "Am I required to do this?" If it is required, you should probably do it, for Uncle Sam or whomever. But that doesn't mean you have to do it *right now*. Ask yourself, "Will there be a better time?"

Third, if you aren't inspired, and it isn't required, ask yourself, "Does anyone desire me to do this?" Here is where many find themselves in a gray area. If a friend asks you to do something and you don't feel inspired to do it, and it's not something you're under contract for, do you go ahead, or do you disappoint them? If your love for them isn't strong enough to inspire you to do it, the deed probably won't be worth much to them anyway. But it's up to you.

Finally, if you aren't inspired, it isn't required, and no one desires you to climb one more mountain, drink one more beer, or wash that floor one more time, then why are you doing it? Maybe you need to sit still for a while and just be.

TRUE ISMS

❧28❧

Truth is simply what is.
How it works is a whole other story!

Truth is overrated. It's no big deal. Everything you can say is possibly true, but some truths are more useful than others. Truth is found not in words, but in this present moment here and now.

Life is so multi-faceted, it's hard to lie if you want to. If you say, "Cows are purple," you can be sure there is a purple cow somewhere west of Toledo you didn't know about. The best most people can manage is half-lies. The only thing worse than a half-lie is a half-truth, and there are plenty of oracles of half-truth around, if you hadn't noticed.

Context is the difference between perception and deception. This realization can either turn you into a complete liar or a completely honest person. It's very humbling to think that all the truths people have written down over the years are only half-truths, but what does that mean to you? If you go around trying to fool and exploit people with words that sound true, you will never help anyone make a real breakthrough and never feel the joy of discovery when you reconnect the strands of the great web and say "Aha!"

If you always speak the truth from where you stand, the people around you will be transformed, whether they are for you or against you, and you will forge a deep, powerful link with the universe, with the core of life, that few have ever experienced. Truth is magic, and those who speak the truth have unspeakable power. Speak the truth from where you stand and you will know a simplicity so fundamental that nothing can fracture it. You will be the hand of God feeding itself. You will create a force field around you that will resonate with something much greater than what you can see with your one little life.

Or you can lie.

❧29❧

It's not what you do, but how you do it.

It's not what you say, it's how you mean it. It's not what you know, but how you see it. It's not what you feel, but how you feel it. It's not what you are, but how you be it.

Any words can be spoken in anger or kindness. Any knowledge can be used to create or destroy. Any feeling can be part of a healing or a suicide. Any action can be beneficial or harmful, depending on the timing and intent. It's not what you are but who you are. For everything there is a season and a time for every purpose under heaven, but now is always the season to be yourself.

✎30✎

If you're not ready and the teacher appears anyway,
go ahead and give it a shot.

A good teacher will never rush you into studying before your time and will accept you as you are and work from there. So the old expression "when the student is ready, the teacher appears" is always true, because a good teacher will only give the student as much as they are ready for, and maybe one step beyond that. If you really weren't ready, the teacher could appear right at your door and you wouldn't notice.

❧31❧

God is not mad at you. Don't let guilt ruin a good sparring round with the Almighty!

Sometimes bad things happen to good people, but that doesn't undermine the theory of cause and effect. It also doesn't mean that the man in the white robe is throwing lightning bolts at you. He may be just giving you practice as a co-worker. Whatever problems you solve today become part of your teaching tomorrow. If people didn't have problems, what would they talk about?

If there is a Father in Heaven, does He get mad and use the belt? Perhaps it's closer to the truth to say God doesn't get mad, He gets even!

If God is Love, then His infinite wisdom understands why we do what we do. It's all part of the plan, and we can choose plan A, plan B, or plan C; first class, coach, or economy. Anger is for those who want to be in control but aren't. If God is the Creator, He is already in control and wants to hand it over to us. Why would He get mad?

If you understood why people did what they do to each other and knew what to do about it, you wouldn't get mad at them, but you might choose to join in the fight if it ends up on your lawn. After all, laws are for everyone.

Life, the Universe, and Everything is a whole, a holistic, dynamic system. It changes but seeks equilibrium, maintaining an overall balance. It gets "even" just as water in a bowl becomes even again after it gets bumped. The universe is that bowl of water and runs largely on cause and effect, as well as other laws that arise out of simple need for things to make sense. Laws save wear and tear on God's imagination—you couldn't stand it any other way.

There is no need for guilt, vengeance, and divine forgiveness over your fate in life when every "mistaken" action gives you an educational and consistent reaction. You touch a hot stove and you get burned—no guilt in that. We are here to be coworkers with the universe, but that also means we can choose to be the opposite, to use free will and be God's sparring partner.

It's true that your "arms are too short to box with God," but some try to kick Him in the shins. It's okay to get mad at God. Just don't stay mad. Madeleine L'Engle once said, "No one ever told me it's not all right to get angry at God. Of course you're allowed, when there is just reason for anger. But you must get through to the other side. I give out a yell, and it's very helpful."

God has to get certain things done, but you don't have to like it.

ᴖ32ᴖ

Be honest but tactful with people.
They're not brainless, but they're not heartless either.

One secret to a simpler life is moderation in all things. True moderation takes guts, because the master of moderation is alone in a class by himself. In the long run, it is still simpler than taking sides.

There will always be misunderstandings and conflicts between people, and communication is the sure answer. But there are two schools of half-truth on how to communicate. Either dazzle 'em with dog duty, or confound 'em with facts; Pamper them with praise, or hit 'em hard with horror. Either approach may work with a "problem person" in an alleyway, but not within the family. You don't help a drunk to seek professional counseling that way, it just pushes them into a cocoon.

Half-truths make the bluntest weapons and the bluntest statements. Don't use truth as a bludgeon to beat your relatives and relationships into submission. They are not heartless. But don't dodge with denial, or damn with faint praise. They're not brainless either.

~33~

Be sincere in your words;
your body language is already spilling the beans.

On the afternoon when writing was first invented, three old codgers went down to the village square to observe what was happening. They were not impressed. "How can you talk to people you can't see?" said one. "How can you tell what people need to hear without reading their reactions, and seeing the look in their face?" the second one said.

"And how can you change your mind once it's written in clay?" said the third. "This is going to cause nothing but trouble." But no one listened, and soon everyone was writing, and they stopped looking at each other and talking through the eyes. They were always looking down at their scrolls.

Of course, many good things have come from writing, but nothing replaces good nonverbal communication. Whether by ESP, intuition, or body language, most people can still sense when they're being lied to or manipulated. They either ignore the feeling (out of diplomacy) or they ignore *you!*

When you speak to babies and animals, they mainly hear your body language. They can't read or write or get lost in the beauty of your logic. They react to you as a person and either trust you or not, the same gut feeling most of us have from time to time. Adults are not so different than babies, so who are you trying to fool, besides yourself? If you believe in what you're saying and say it well, you will go home in their hearts. If you don't believe what you're saying, you can coat it with syrup, but it will still go in one end and out the other. We can't digest that which is artificial.

✌34✌

If you really want to amaze people, tell the truth.

Why wait until you have a nervous breakdown before you start telling it like it is? Call 'em as you see 'em, and let other people go crazy instead. Only when we have nothing left to lose do we finally lose our attachment to appearances, and only then do we gain the treasure of vulnerability. The best comedians (and drunks) are hugely funny because they tell it straight from the heart, without the flowers.

First imagine what you could say to people if you had nothing whatsoever to lose...now imagine that said in the light of compassion and love. That's the way the sages have always spoken to people—no differently now than 5,000 years ago. Can you imagine living like that today?

The difference between the simple sage and the priest is that priests worry about attendance. The priest chooses his words carefully so people will come back next Sunday. On the other hand, when the sage unveils the truth, only the truth-seekers return. The rest are outraged. How can you speak the truth about the human condition to those who are responsible for it and expect them to come to your next meeting? The only honest man is one who has learned to live without friends, but in the end, no one has more trusted friends than he.

❧35❧

Truth, like water, seeks its own level.

Truth is fluid because life is fluid. If you wish to resonate with truth, speak to people in the moment, for the moment. Speak in response to life, and be one with it. The most powerful dreams merely express what is happening, but with insight; The wisdom of the creator reaches us through such dreams and through each other by describing, and in a way each of us can understand. Words of truth don't tell you what to do but help you see. We are truth, but we leave ourselves to go looking for it. We can stir things up by lying and deceiving, but the truth balances everything out in the end. Some talkers paint the bright picture of life, others a dark picture, but the picture is the same until you brush on the paint.

Listen to people to tell how they're thinking, but watch their actions to see how they feel. Great liars are heaven-sent, because they remind us how superficial words are, and how we fool ourselves with them. They don't change things. Some lies have persisted for hundreds of years, but they still don't change what people really think and do—they adapt to lies like they adapt to bunions. Perhaps our true identity falls somewhere in the huge abyss between what we want, say, and do—where thinking meets feeling and fact.

SIMPLICITY PATTERNS

༺ 36 ༺

A sense of wonder excuses much ignorance.

Wonder is the natural reaction to reality, for both spirit and nature are awe inspiring. Only machines are predictable. If your life is too predictable, avoid machines for a while, including cars, phones, or TV sets.

The ignorant person is one who either hasn't had a chance to learn, or whose learning process is blocked. Unblock the learning process, give them time and space, and eventually ignorance will give way to wisdom. But it takes a certain quality to overcome hardships along the way, and that quality is a sense of wonder.

Ignorance can be ignored, but a sense of wonder is wonderful.

Wonder is where the open heart and the open mind become united in a blissful conjugation. An open mind without an open heart leads us down a hundred dead ends, and life becomes complex and wearying. An open heart without an open mind leads us into parochialism, provincialism, and bigotry. With both the heart and mind open, you can go anywhere and do anything, overcome any ignorance and still be on the simple road. A sense of wonder is a gift, a birthright from the universe, the key to the kingdom, which little children have. If you run out of this kind of wealth, go borrow a sense of wonder from your neighborhood four-year-old. It will do wonders for your senses.

⁓37⁓

Focus on yourself and be tense, focus on others and relax.

In everything you do there is a gift for you and a gift for others. Look for those gifts, especially the gift for others.

Happiness is simple, misery is complicated. If you want to be happy, focus on the simple and relax. If you want to be miserable, focus on the complicated and worry. Of course, life's not that simple—actually, it's pretty complicated. So how can one find happiness?

Maybe the answer is that *one* can't, but *two* might. Happiness comes when there is a balance between "self" and "other." The way to make someone miserable is to put them on the defensive and make things as complicated as possible, and above all, make sure there is no "other" person or noble cause they can help along the way. Get them to focus only on *them*, and they will consume themselves with anxious thought.

There is a lot of unhappiness in the world right now. People have already been trained to think only of themselves, and now life has suddenly gotten much more complicated, because of an economic downturn. The leaders blame the people and the people blame the leaders. For this reason, it especially important to keep things simple and not blame yourself too much. Guilt and narcissism are extremes; try to find the middle.

Guilt is a way of making people think about themselves. Blame yourself, and others will follow. Charitable acts probably do more for the giver than for the "needy," as they rechannel anxieties to the problems of others. Try to make others happy out of a sense of guilt, and more guilt follows. Try to make others happy for the sake of enjoying the interaction, and more joy will follow.

Another way to make someone miserable is to give them a puzzle that can't be solved and make a personal issue out of it. Get them to accept it as a litmus test of honor or shame.

Millions of people around the world enjoy solving puzzles as a way of relaxing, and the more complicated the better. Some of the most complicated ones were thought up in ancient Egypt, and during the Islamic Renaissance, so puzzles are nothing new. The point of that kind of puzzle is to get the mind to disengage from the self and wrap in fascination around the puzzle, entering into the great impersonal reality of the divine mind. Focusing on a Celtic Meander, or a Hindu Mandala, can bring the same profound sense of peace as an Arabic puzzle, for the same reason. It keeps the worrying watchdog out of the way. But reverse the process, set the mind puzzling on itself, and peace is destroyed.

The tricky thing about a gift is that is has to be given, not stolen. It is not self-sacrifice unless it is voluntary. If you feel pushed into self-sacrifice, you are probably a victim and not a hero. Generosity makes relationships simpler, but when a generous person becomes a door mat, complications follow. Allegiance without free will, teamwork without volunteers, charity without choice is not heroic, it is slavery.

∽38∽

Live like a trial lawyer: never admit fault, allow no room for argument, squeeze confessions out of people, box others in—and end up behind bars...of loneliness.

Some people actually do this and wonder why their lives get so complicated. In an actual trial there is always another lawyer in the room, so there is a balance of power. Each attorney focuses on the pluses of his own client and that keeps things simple. In real life, if your friends feel they have to have their lawyer with them to talk to you, they'll leave and get him, or just leave.

In a courtroom, everyone is following the same rule book, which keeps things simple as well. In real life, no one is following the same rule book, everyone is following their own heart—it makes things complicated, but only if you try to control people. Allow others the right to their own rule book— not everyone had your mother and father for parents.

In a real courtroom, most of us can't leave when we want to. In real life, if you start imitating Perry Mason over every mistake, most people will cast their verdict with their feet—and leave. Become a lawyer of the heart and you are courting disaster.

❧ 39 ❧

There will always be cynics.
Don't try to join them, or cure them.

Cynicism is something like STD's, only it is spread by promiscuous talking. It is a deficiency of the spiritual immune system. It often comes from hanging around the wrong people, and needing too much. It comes from being either too selfish or too unselfish, from trying too hard or not enough. It comes from doing too much too soon, or not enough too late.

Many cynics are optimists on the rebound. Many cynics are people who have tried to do the impossible at the wrong time and failed. People who run away from personal problems and try to tame the world without mastering themselves first often get into a heap of complications, and end up cynical. Cynicism is armor for people without skin. You need to build up to your heroism slowly and develop a thick skin before you take on the world. And remember this note of wisdom: all that armor can be noisy.

⋅⋅ 40 ⋅⋅

When it comes to simplicity, Nature is the greatest guru.
Where do you think the holy men go for their best ideas?

If you want to help people, first get as far away from them as possible. If you need help in opening the heart, go to the woods. If you need healing and comfort, go to the woods. If you want to open the inner eye, if you are looking for new ideas, if you are looking for wisdom teachings, go to the woods.

Respect the earth and all life on it— whatever made you made it. Nature is the mold into which you were poured. Nature is everything outside of your own narrow opinions, fantasies, constructions, theories, and bigotries. Nature is the thing that doesn't change when we change. Nature is universal principles in action. Nature is not a hypothesis, it is proof. What a piece of work is Man— a piece in a great biological machine.

Man is not the measure of all things—merely the measurer. Humankind is not the inheritor of the earth—merely the executor of the Will. We are part mortal and part divine—but then, so is a slug. God created Nature in Her own image. You are what Nature thinks you are, not the other way around.

The worlds of spiritual and artistic vision, of pure feelings, ideas, prophecies and prayers, transcend the laws of our physical earth, and the laws of society. And yet these worlds are part of our natural, internal environment and have laws of their own and landscapes that are as timeless as the mountains. Follow their teachings and you will realize a world of Nature that embraces all of the earth, humanity, the Soul, and God. It is not a world we never made, nor a figment of our imagination. It just is.

❧ 41 ❧

You can only borrow time, or waste it. You can never save it. Short cuts are seldom the last word in anything.

Don't be minute-wise and hour-foolish.

Time is like the rain. We drink its water, wash with it, play with it, but we are always borrowing it. Eventually, it goes back to the earth. As long as we don't pollute it, we're not wasting a drop. Even water poured on the desert will find its way to a cloud.

Time is a gift like the rain. It flows around you for your use. You can store it, splash in it, use it sparingly, or drink thereof, but time is never wasted unless you pollute it with your habits, your angers, and your fears.

There are two kinds of time: cosmic time, which is cyclic, and biological time, which is rhythmic. Some so-called "high cultures" favor a fixed, cyclic view of time, based on celestial mechanics, but the biological sense of time possessed by the earth-based peoples is equally valid, equally useful. Truly successful people are able to reconcile the two and waste nothing. I've met only a few who can do this, but I believe that a hundred years from now, such wisdom will be common.

Don't be second-wise and lifetime-foolish.

Time is a flow of atoms, like the flow of air through a flute. In the hands of an artist, the notes ebb and flow in a dance of time, as opposed to the "strict time" of the metronome. On the invisible level, the air particles within the flute compress and relax, always balancing out in the end. Life in the hands of a true artist is also a dance of time, compressing and relaxing, following the natural line of the story.

Don't confine your private life to the clock tower. The movement of the sun and the stars is only a metronome click to the music of the heart, which dances and sweeps to the pulses of the soul.

❧ 42 ❧

*Complexity comes from living
beyond the means of your wisdom.*

Wisdom means knowing when to begin something, when to stop, and when to backtrack. It means knowing when to go straight, when to turn, and when to dance a jig in the road; when to shout, when to talk, and when to just observe; when to risk, when to wait, and when to hide in the sand; when to play, when to pass, and when to cheat at cards. All these things are acquired only by a mixture of experience and intuition, and, once in a while, by observing the mistakes of others. You can't buy wisdom, even in the New Age.

Wisdom is power; not a power to create or destroy, but only to sustain. Still, it is a great power, the only one that doesn't corrupt. If you have it, you can avoid complications.

If you don't have much wisdom, you can still avoid complications by stretching what little you have, going slowly, step by step, outside of your familiar territory, until you make it your own. Run wildly into uncharted experiences beyond the charts of your wisdom, and life will get complicated.

It is wise, then, to be wise. Once you have infinite wisdom, you can go anywhere with grace and ease, and carry your simple-hearted life with you wherever you go.

❧ 43 ❧

Love all, trust few.

This may sound harsh, but it will make your life simpler. People confuse love and trust, at least until they have children. People are usually afraid to love because they are afraid to trust. If you separate the two, then can you love everyone, because you certainly can't trust everyone.

People who confuse love with trust have miserable relationships because the other person has to be perfect, and no one is perfect. A balanced attitude towards trust leads to a balanced love. We need to trust many people in our life, but the boundaries of that trust should be mutually understood. We need to trust our doctor, our dentist, our mechanic, and our teachers, (maybe even our lawyer) to do their jobs to the best of their ability, "to earn their bucks," or the fabric of society breaks down. Even that trust is relative.

What no one agrees on is how far to trust our friends, gurus, lovers, and spouses. We don't have proper boundaries for that kind of trust. If our mechanic is caught in a domestic scandal, we still trust him with our car. But if our guru does the same, do we still trust him (or her) with leading us to higher realities? No one seems to agree. If we feel violated by that, are we then asking the guru to be perfect according to our standards? To fit into our society? It sounds like a recipe for disappointment to me.

People who say everything is perfect, no one needs forgiveness, overlook the prevalence of this love *vs* trust problem. If the disappointment is outside the boundaries of our trustbond, we need to be understanding, but if it's within those boundaries, we need to forgive; not a God-like redemption of the Soul, but a renewal of that contract within, and it should be expressed in some way.

Preventative medicine applies here, too. The old adage "put your trust in writing" is a good idea, if only to clarify the boundaries of trust. If you trust someone to do something, they should by all means be told about it.

PROBLEM SOLVING

❧ 44 ❧

Life is like baseball. Even if the last time you made an error was St. Louis, 1968, you're not infallible. Admit it and relax.

You run out every grounder, but sometimes you get to first base and sometimes you don't.

Being a perfectionist is a mistake, so if you're trying for that 100% statistic, you've already blown it. Strive for perfection when it matters, but sometimes it doesn't matter, and sometimes, you're better off making mistakes. (Some practice in the batting cage never hurt anyone.) The important thing is learning, and the perfectionist who won't take a risk is a poor learner. Perfectionists are mainly singles hitters and seldom make Grand Slams. Home run batters are strikeout kings, they risk all for the chance at a round trip ticket.

First realize that you are not going to reach every goal you set on the first try, and that's a good thing. Then realize that others can't be forced to reach your goals for you either, and that's a good thing, too.

Learn to forgive yourself and then learn to forgive others for not being born perfect, and life will be happier and simpler. Then, once you are feeling glad to be alive, you may realize there was nothing to forgive in the first place, that everything happens for a reason, and the reason is to learn and to grow. But you have to go through the forgiving stage first or it doesn't count.

✌ 45 ✌

No one is wrong all the time either. As my mother used to say, "Even a stopped clock is right once a day!" (That's twice a day, mom!)

Everything has its place, and truer words were never spoken than those that said, "For everything, turn, turn, there is a season, turn, turn, and a time for every purpose under heaven." As the Catskill comic said, "Timing is everything." Every dog has his day. Even the most painfully misfit person has that moment in the sun when only they could do it right. A kid on my block who was always in some kind of trouble or another went to Vietnam, became a medic, and came back with dozens of medals and saved countless lives. His "troubles" taught him to be fearless. We all have moments of destiny. Find that moment now.

❧46❧

Don't waste time by doing things in the wrong order.

Simplicity comes from ordering events in a natural sequence. But in a 3-D, non-linear world, what is "order?" I can't tell you, but it's certainly not a straight line. The biosphere, which is elegantly simple, is in want of a straight line anywhere. Simplicity is the evolutionary direction of the spirit, and there's no end. Once you begin improving your sequencing, you'll never run out of ways to improve it until life is reduced to a simple circle again. A straight line misses 359 degrees. The Algonquin elders used to move clockwise like the sun—because, if you want to see everything, the best route between two points (and back) is a circle.

Move around cautiously when you are unfamiliar, gather information in circular ways, stalk your destiny like a hunter. If you are going to enter with pride, let that pride be based on something other than ignorance.

Move boldly in a straightish line when you have seen the whole circle and know where to step. Successful people who make short, bold strokes are like chess masters who have been around for many years and know all the moves. But you may first have to absorb their knowledge before you can copy their actions.

~47~

The problem is not that people think too much, but that they want too much, and it causes confused thinking.

So many people who are into a spiritual thing are into an anti-intellectual thing as well, but there is nothing bad about the stream of thoughts running through your head as long as you can turn it off. Thoughts help you solve problems, they help you survive in this world where you hope to be of service, they help you evaluate and understand what is happening to you spiritually and help put things in relationship with one another. All the bad things that are said about thought are really said about confused thought, which is a very different thing.

Confused thoughts arise when thoughts are not free but are subject to desire. We are sentient beings, first and foremost; we are beings that are capable of thought and feeling and likely to think and feel at any moment. This is natural and good. Our lives are powered forward by desire and steered by thought. When that desire dominates thought and fact, thoughts try to accomodate desire and become confused.

Some of our basic desires are for identity, love, security, finality, self-esteem, justice, and power. Each has its place, but each contain the ability to skew thought if taken to extremes.

If the desire for identity dominates, we may choose to think ourselves into an easy, limited role in life that "has all the answers" and is a straight-jacket to soul. We may become self-conscious and stiff.

If the desire for love is too great, we may choose not to see the facts and consequently, may avoid the hard decisions that might lose us our friends. We might become over-protective of loved ones, and not let them grow.

If the desire for security is too great, we may rationalize about the conditions in our own life so that we don't have to change things, or even make arguments why things should not be changed.

If our desire for finality is too great, we may get hide-bound in our thoughts and be unable to change or see the other side of the coin. We may refuse what spirit brings us.

If the desire for self-esteem is too great, we may be unable to admit that what we do isn't working and twist the facts around as part of our denial.

If the desire for justice is too great, we may live our lives out in a state of anger, unable to see the higher justice, unable to wait for the wheel to come around for us again, stopping the wheel of life, of our own destiny.

Lastly, if the desire for power is too great, we may desperately try all the above, and to our own detriment, trying to justify our thirst for control, rather than releasing it to spirit. These extremes are significant. They can each stop our spiritual growth, which eventually leads to darkness and destruction until it is corrected.

These are the kinds of extremes that we should be on guard against. If we find such thoughts, it is not necessary to destroy them, nor is it necessary to destroy the desires that caused them to enlarge. It is simply necessary to put thought and feeling into balance with fact once again.

❦48❧

When in doubt, clean house.

I know I'm not the first or the last to think of this, but you can always get a feeling of direction from cleansing something that belongs to you before making a decision, be it your car, your house, your shop, office, or your own grungy body. Looking at a just-cleaned desk or table strikes a sympathetic chord in the mind and suddenly everything seems much clearer. Call it suburban voodoo.

Another advantage to housecleaning, which has nothing to do with "cleanliness is next to Godliness" (which is dubious since God invented dirt in the first place), is that it's a convenient way to vent one's anger and frustration at the world. All that mess, dirt, and grime can easily be mistaken for boss, wife, husband, or "those people," when in an angry state of mind. That anger comes in handy when aimed at piles of papers, dusty cars, or scraggly weed patches, and when you're done, you may find that your mind has gotten squeaky clean as well.

෴49෴

*You can't take care of others
unless you take care of yourself.*

Nothing is more dangerous than people with "nothing but good intentions."
It takes more than good intentions to take charge in an emergency. It takes
wisdom, courage, and years of experience.

Of course, good years of experience come from years of good intentions,
but there are a lot of bruises along that route. When some people get religion,
in the throes of surrender, they throw all their tools out the window, and then
expect God to save the world through them. God answers, "What was that
you just threw out the window? Was that my good set of tools? My hammer?
My saw? What the ____ you doin'? Now I gotta save you!" But the person
doesn't always want to hear.

Sometimes, a person has been on the wrong road so long, they really do
need to surrender to a new set of tires. If you reach the end of the road, let
go and let God show you how to live your own life, not the person's next
to you. The surrender strategy works. It leads to the self-sufficiency strategy,
which leads to the helping-others strategy. Since kindness is the best strategy
for love and happiness—surrender, regroup, and serve, and you will be
happy.

⌐50⌐

Things that must be done at all costs
usually cost about that much.

This is one law that Murphy overlooked, but it's true, and you can prove it to yourself, although I sincerely hope you don't. There is a special law of relativity that says "The more you push, the less you get back." It only works under conditions of vanity, ego, attachment, anger, frustration, or greed. To confront the entire universe from a position of power, which is what you're doing when you say, "This way or else," is to ask for a humbling experience. The universe is intrigued by such challenges. "At any cost? Have it your way." When you are so involved in illusions that you think one thing is more important than everything else, you are lost. That's called attachment to circumstances. The fate of the world may turn on one pediment, but it's probably not the one you are standing on.

The means determine the ends. Garbage in, garbage out. The ends can only justify the means in hindsight, never as a way of doing business, because it usually doesn't work. Better to make the means sufficiently worthy of celebrating today or there'll be no end to the mourning. I would go as far as to say that since life is a circle, there is no separating ends and means; every point on the circle is both. Try to make the whole circle strong, not just one isolated point.

❧51❧

Leave time for the unexpected to happen,
but always bring a book to read in case it doesn't.

The art of finding ever new ways to conserve time is a key to simpler living, but if you look back and realize you have left no time for reality to seep in, it may be too much of a good thing. When people discover a new trick, such as time management, they are often over-zealous in the beginning. I bet the first person to discover you could stack rocks to make a stone wall probably walled themselves in. No matter, just pull some of those rocks down and make some windows for yourself. Make time holes in your schedule, just in case life has some original ideas. If you want to be a coworker with creation, you can go more than halfway, but don't get so close you step on creation's toes—allow it to share in the decision making.

There really is a right time for everything, and it may not always seem convenient. You'll know when the right time comes—after it left. You'll look back and see that everything happened when it had to, at just the right time. If you're still worried that leaving some breathing room in your wall of appointments will make you inefficient, bring a book to read. If that's still not efficient enough, bring a self-help book to read. If all else fails, spend some quality time with the universe.

✋ 52 ✋

Just because you're responsible for what happens to your life doesn't mean you're to blame for everything.

The issue of responsibility versus blame is a hot topic right now, and it's caused a lot of confusion. Many people are just now breaking away from the old world consciousness where the rule was blame first and ask questions later. Guilt has been the glue that's held western society together for the last 1,000 years, and the church, government, and legal system have been painted with it, even education, and are slow to become unstuck. Unfortunately, as guilt is rejected, instead of embracing the responsibility principle, establishments are becoming unglued instead. They have gone from guilt to greed and are no closer to responsibility.

Blame is a debt that you aren't allowed to pay off. It's as if someone tricked you into stealing their money and then refused to take the money or your apologies back. It's not simple, efficient, or fair. As a matter of fact, it sounds a little self-destructive.

Responsibility is a whole different matter. It's borrowing and lending with the understanding that you have to give back everything sooner or later. Taking responsibility means that no matter what hardships may follow your decisions, you will eventually balance it out as best as you can, whether it be a matter of time, energy, or work, love, or money. Gandhi once recommended to a Hindu man who killed a Muslim that he adopt a Muslim boy and raise him as his own, only as a Muslim. That's an example of long-term responsibility.

The New Age types tell us that we are responsible for everything that happens in our life, good or bad. For someone from the old school, this sounds like "you are to blame for everything." This is not the case. What it means is that we are always somehow involved in the decision, and so many things that seem negative, we actually chose, and chose wrong for a good reason, however hard that reason is to see. Although there may be a good reason for hardship, we still try to resolve the hardship, but we try to learn from it as well. When we understand the reason for the hardship and accept it, we can take responsibility for mistakes.

Mistakes usually have reasons, and they often lie in the realm of the subconscious; the psychological and the spiritual. When we heal the wound in the subconscious, the mistake stops happening. Blaming just makes the wound worse. Every living person over the age of 21 is the survivor of an honest mistake. They made it through, and so can you.

I can take responsibility for the world as it is, as long as I accept it *more or less* as it is. I can take responsibility for myself as I am, as long as I can accept myself *more or less* as I am. If I see myself and my world in a negative light, however, and can't accept it, I can't take responsibility for it without taking blame for it as well, because it seems to be more of a debt than I can make good on.

COWORKING

❧53❧

Think clearly. God has to have something to work with.

Putting the cart before the horse usually indicates an ignorance of cause and effect, or a lack of concern for the horse. Simplicity comes from understanding these subtleties.

There's nothing less cosmic than being disorganized: the very word cosmos means "order." The question is, does my order match the cosmic order? Dictators think so, Sages know so. The Hair-Brained presume so and the Bean Counters presume not so. The Hair-Brained like to excuse themselves as following a higher cosmic order, and the Bean Counters like to think there is no cosmic order, which is job security for them. Dictators upset the cosmic order, and Sages restore the cosmic order. Either way, if cosmos is order, there must be a way to take it all in and still think fairly coherently. Be neither for nor against, but don't be afraid to categorize.

Make a list of everything you need to do to reach your goal, then put it in chronological order when you're finished. Pin it to the wall and forget it.

Make a list of everything you do that helps you reach your goal and another list of everything that prevents you from reaching your goal. Put them in priority order, pin them to the wall, and forget them.

Self-discipline does not imply there is something wrong with your self that requires punishment. The word discipline comes from the Old English word for learning and comprehension skills, but sometime during monastic history it turned to mean "being corrected," and then came to mean "punishment and control." Self-discipline implies you are the master of your fate. It also means you can correct yourself. We all make mistakes, but that doesn't mean there's something wrong with us; the questions on the test were not always covered in class. Keep trying to put things in order, as if you were the secretary of God, even if there is always a thunderstorm in His office.

❧54❧

Be a coworker with Creation.
If all else fails, let Creation do all the work.

Some people refer to God, the Creator, as "He." But God to me is an invisible sun stretching from eternity to eternity at the center of the spiritual world. Out of its powerful heart are tossed spiritual stars, souls, and spiritual planets, and the inner planes, and this world is a reflection of those higher realms. Our own sun is a reflection of that center, in that everything comes from it and will return to it some day. We and all the plants look to it for light and warmth and sustenance.

Our sun is rather bright but not so intelligent. God, however, is beyond bright and is filled with love, intelligence, wisdom, and more and manifests this through the mysterious figures that come to us in dreams, visions, and contemplations. Every ancient culture speaks of these great beings who have become mouthpiece-masks of the invisible God.

To be a coworker with creation, learn to chat with the Creator on a most intimate basis. If you can't seem to catch Its attention, try whispering into Its ear. Whispering out loud is very powerful. Be a conscious channel for the Creator, not a zombie. Take responsibility for what comes through you and make it your own. Your song is part of the music of the spheres, but it's still your lyrics. When we as artists are divinely inspired, we still sign our work.

If you can't work with the abstraction of talking to an invisible sun, or you have an aversion to father-figures, talk to life all around you, for that, too, is God, the Creator, in manifestation.

❧55❧

Ask and it shall be given. But it matters when and how you ask for it. Timing is everything.

Why do I always forget to seek, knock, and ask for guidance? Don't answer that! Seriously, it does seem that some people's prayers are heard and others' don't seem to be. Why is it that when some ask the universe a question, they get an answer, while others get a busy signal? Since I don't believe there is a double standard in this, the difference must lie in how we ask. When you ask Dad for The Keys to the Universe, you have to really mean it. You should also know how to drive.

It really doesn't matter how good or bad you think you are. This is your universe. If you can clear your mind enough to know what you want, you can tap into a resonance with reality and bring it to you.

The first law of asking is that you have to need it. The second law of asking is that you have to want it and mean it. The third law of asking is that it must be good for the whole, and in harmony with that which already is. It helps if the asking is on behalf of someone else, but only on their request, or if their fate and yours are intertwined. When you get your answer, again declare that you will use what you learned for the good of the whole.

The fourth law of asking is that you must leave it open ended as to how the answer will come or how the goal will be reached. Leave the universe room to bow out gracefully. Don't make ultimatums.

The fifth law of asking is to seek the truth. Don't say, "I want to know the truth as long as it's this one." Drop your attachments and fears and be ready for the truth.

The sixth law of asking is that you throw yourself wholly into it. Be willing to exchange your life, if necessary, for the truth, for understanding, for guidance. Offer your heart as a trade for what you seek. Make yourself the sacrifice. The seventh law of asking is to be humble. You can never be sure if what you heard is what God really said.

❧56❧

*Accept yourself for who you are now,
and only then can you change.*

You can only start a journey from where you stand today. This sounds obvious enough, but when you no longer have your feet on the ground, it doesn't seem to matter where you stand. People get lost in so many theories about what it means to work with higher consciousness, they forget about where they were going in their own journey on earth. Don't forget that your personality is part of who you are as a person, with all the warts and bunions. Stand in your own shoes and walk the first mile, no matter how tight the fit.

Meaning comes out of relationship, and so it's important to deepen your understanding of relationship, whether with family, friends, the world, or the spirit. They are all just different facets of one thing, relating. People tend to be good at either the "higher" or "lower" kinds of relating, but seldom both. People either run from human relating and bury themselves in the big, fuzzy picture, or they can't bear the big picture and bury themselves in humanity. Either way, as long as part of the picture is missing, part of the meaning of life will be missing as well.

You're already playing hide and seek with yourself. Find out where you've been hiding, and flush yourself out of the bushes. Accept yourself for who you've been, and then look up. What's the next step? Which way do you want to go? If you don't want to know your self, what is this enlightenment you were just seeking? How can you lose yourself in bliss when you never earned a self to begin with? Get a life first, and then tell me you're prepared to meet death.

☙57❧

Jealousy is a war on God within the heart and leads to war among people.

Jealousy is the one emotion we can most do without. Jealousy is man's way of saying to God, "To hell with your divine plan for me, I like the divine plan you gave *him* better!" Jealousy is not a lofty belief in equality, but an overlooking of the equality in the law of karma that is already fleecing all of us.

There are many kinds of jealousy, and there isn't much good in any of them, but I'll list them, just in case you want to try one anyway.

First there is the kind where you want what the other person has so much, you drop all your goals in life, and go off in pursuit of something similar. Monkey see, monkey do.

The second is the kind where you love equality so much you are eager to cut anyone down to size who has more on the ball than you do. This could include robbing them of what you don't have, injuring them, belittling them, breaking whatever it is they earned for themselves, or just feeling like you want to scratch their eyes out. A variation on this is when feel you are the only person who has a certain something and you want to keep it that way, "incumbency," as they say in Washington.

The third is a combination of both. You want to "get what they got," and break theirs too.

The fourth is possessiveness, where you feel entitled to exclusive control over someone else, and the universe doesn't cooperate. This is really pre-jealousy—you're afraid someone else is about to have what you would like to have. Such preemptive strikes are meant to prevent this "inequality" from happening, but they usually backfire.

Every once in a while, jealousy inspires someone to achieve something beyond what they thought they could do, but I suspect this enviable result is rather rare.

ᔒ58ᔔ

Don't underestimate what you can do in five minutes,
don't overestimate what you can do in five years.

We have the ability to compress time into short little bundles, but we have to compensate somewhere else—something to do with the law of conservation of energy.

In five minutes you can: read a page or two of a book, make a list of "things to do today," practice each of the major scales on piano (if you're already very good), make one obligatory phone call, clean a window, scrub one table top, wash 1/4 of a kitchen floor, hug your significant other, write a short letter, do a very short contemplation, race around the block twice, do 50 pushups, 100 jumping jacks, hang up half a load of laundry, dust two shelves, take a quick shower...or watch one segment of commercials on TV and learn nothing.

If you're interested in time management, one of the most important things to realize is that there are many activities you can also do while performing the above: boil water, run the washer, run the computer printer, or listen to audio literature, talk on the phone, think, run the vacuum.

On the other hand, please realize that the stride you hit five minutes before you leave for the airport is not meant to be kept up for five years. You can't really save time, you just borrow it.

Big things take time. Rome wasn't built in five years, the American Revolution took more than five, the cathedrals of Europe usually took fifty years to build, most businesses need five years to begin to make a profit. Even if you can "do it all" in five years, you may need to rest up afterwards; In

October 1962, the Beatles first single was released. Five years later, they had already written most of their songs as a band—but they needed lots of rest afterwards. Gorbachev became Premiere of the USSR in March of 1985, and five years later, his reign was all but over. Time is very flexible, but demands respect.

☙59❧

Spirit moves in an instant, the heart moves in time.
Move in heart time and you'll live forever in that instant.

People get confused sometimes between the heart and the soul, but what is the difference? The heart changes slowly like the phases of the moon, the soul is always there unchanging, like the sun, hiding behind the clouds and then suddenly appearing. Slow down your life and the heart grows strong. Expand your horizons and the soul grows bright.

The heart creeps forward step by step like a baby, wave by wave like the tide, but the soul moves swift as lightning, or an ocean storm, and acts with masterful self-assuredness.

How do you strike a balance between the strong heart and the bright soul? Move in heart time but without limits. Embrace all of life every instant, but do it from where you stand.

⚏60⚏

Work out your personal problems with all seriousness,
but be able to drop them at any time.
(i.e. Don't worry, be happy.)

If you can't drop it, you don't have a problem, it has you! Some problems are solved by dropping the subject, especially if you've become rather well versed in what you're dropping.

Robert Gass once observed that most childhood-related personal problems are like an itch you can scratch and scratch but that never goes away. You need to work through your father problem or your mother problem or your sibling problem, but don't get hooked on that emotional baggage. You can heal a lot of it, but it never goes away completely. It's part of our ballast that keeps us at the bottom of the ocean of love we're in.

The best thing to do about a problem is to return to it whenever you feel you have a fresh perspective to give to it and drop it again as soon as it gets stale. Examine that old wound only when you have a new healer in your life, a new perspective, a new inspiration, a new power. Otherwise you will be like the person who gets addicted to scratching their own poison ivy. It just gets worse that way, it never heals.

The ability to look squarely at pain gives you a survival advantage over the average person, but if you can't let go until it's 100% finished, that strength can become a "tragic flaw." There is no 100% solution to the human condition, so if you can't drop it and walk in the sunshine, you're stuck in the darkness.

INNER PATHWAYS

∾61∾

Trust your higher self, not your compulsions.

A teacher once said, "Never trust the human state of consciousness." Why not? I've come to the working hypothesis that there are seeds of addiction somewhere in the body, a disease that everyone has, but each has it for something different. Likewise, the human consciousness contains seeds of compulsions that are self-destructive. We are attracted to the things we're allergic to and become dependent on that which weakens us. If there was ever a time when such wasn't the case, it was thousands of years ago before we started being so complicated.

On the other hand, our minds and bodies are vehicles for the divine. If the divine wants a miracle to happen, who does "it" have to turn to other than us? Why make a rock fly when it's much simpler to get some human to throw it?" We (including animals) are the only available help, and when we become the catapult, amazing things happen. It's the higher self, the Soul body, the spark of God that is the actual conduit for the universal life force, but it has to use our messy minds, our motor mouths, and our bloated bodies to manifest!

The problem is that we can't just put our personalities in a suitcase, like Charlie McCarthy on tour, and let this universal force do everything it wants to do through us. It never works for long. That's like putting potato salad in a box and letting it sit for a year. If you stop working with your human consciousness and put it in a box for five years, I'd be afraid to open the box. Leave it there long enough and that box will start opening, or perhaps even dissolving, by itself. You have to work on yourself, and your compulsions, just don't get compulsive about it. Keep improving the human state of consciousness slowly and surely, and spend lots of time being a channel too. This higher self would love to see the lower self get its act together—slowly and patiently for a change.

❧62❧

Life is an iceberg, 90% hidden.
Keep looking for the answers beneath the surface.

Keeping the outer life simple and productive is the foundation of a strong spiritual life and takes a lot of time. If we sleep eight hours a day, we may spend eight hours at work and eight hours in spiritual or community service, to keep the three in balance. Attention on the outer life keeps us well-grounded and able to be of service when needed. The reason we incarnated was not to see how long we could defy the experience of incarnation. We need to live it to the fullest as if we really meant to come here, and as if this living were not a bizarre accident, but a part of some divine plan.

Living every day as a team player on earth is essential. But let me add that everyday reality is just the tip of the iceberg and does not explain itself. For every mountain there are a thousand in other dimensions. For every visible teacher, there are a thousand unseen teachers dwelling on other planes. For every piece of music composed, there are a thousand that remain unchosen. A thousand vast landscapes await those who cling to a single vista here on this world. For the one who can access those inner worlds, the amount of information available is staggering.

The future already exists, so clearly that people can see it and even change it. Past lives can be viewed in the inner memory. The amount of telepathy and communication that goes on beyond this material world is amazing and helps cause much of what happens in our life.

Certain people who have had near-death experiences have come back many times more loving, many times more intelligent, confident, even more educated. Some come back with healing powers, some with a mission, some seeing the future. But all will tell you this: this world we see here is just the tip of a vast iceberg. We are sitting on a gold mine every day of our lives.

⟡ 63 ⟡

*There's only one way to avoid pitfalls—
walk close with God.*

Let's face it, life is dangerous. Like a good story, life is a series of "First the bad news, then the good news," with conflicts and resolutions. The important thing is not how you look falling down, but what you learn from the experience on the way up. Are you learning to walk, or are you just learning how to have skinned knees?

Life will always have its share of problems—no matter how high up the mountain you go, there will always be loose rocks. Given that, is there any reason to live a life of misery, or would you really like to solve even the most difficult situations with a certain aplomb and grace?

Pitfalls are usually hidden. That's what makes them pitfalls. There are always unknown dangers in any situation and always unknown aspects to any known danger. You can't rely on logic alone to get you through unscathed, because you never have all the facts. You have to trust inner guidance and intuition. You can always tell people who don't trust their instincts, they only go for the sure thing, they go with the statistics. The spiritual people trust the force, Luke.

Everyone has an inner link with the universe, and you can chat with it like your neighbor or best friend. It can tell you just enough to keep you safe, but hardly a word more. Its word may tell you to move to the right, then left, then back the other way, so you have to keep listening, but you will be guided along.

I believe that those with their spiritual ears open can get through a whole life without major personal disaster, but that it gets more and more difficult as you take on more of life in your charge. Eventually, even the most devoted among us misses a cue or says, "Let's just find out for once" and falls into the pit. Enjoy the ride. If you ache, it means you're living, and perhaps learning with your whole being, something you never would have discovered if you had stuck to Plan A.

ᴄ64ᴗ

Visualize your way through problems,
using light and sound, not just action.

Someone once asked me if I knew of a book that would change their luck—a startling question. I gave them a book on visualization. If you can visualize yourself in a place, you can get there. If you can visualize the steps to get there as well, it will be simple.

Luck is either karmic or habitual. If it's karmic, it means you earned it. It can't be changed except through changing the consciousness. If it is habitual, it is created by subconscious habits and fixed patterns that can be changed through visualization, therapy, fasting, or asking a higher power for help.

Most people visualize in a very limited way and don't learn anything new. Open-ended visualization, on the other hand, brings you to a place you've never been before. You are no longer just mocking up the images, but something is happening to you. It is not only surprising, there is usually a lesson in it.

Open-ended visualization can go beyond just moving actors around on your inner stage; you can use light and sound to represent positive forces in your life. You can use an orange light to represent energizing forces, yellow to represent clarity of mind, green light to represent soothing and harmonizing forces, blue light to represent spiritual forces, teachings, and blessings, or purple light to represent blissful or magical feelings. You can use such lights to send these energies to others or to yourself, and soon they appear in your dreams and, in unexpected ways, in your daily life, which expands your whole scope of action.

Sound can be used in the same way. You can imagine beautiful symphonic sounds to relax you or uplift you during contemplation, to link you to "higher" spheres. You can also use songs and chants, or monosyllables such as OM or HU to cleanse your aura. This may sound rather "new age" but since our subconscious minds are often creating negative, paranoid fantasies and attracting "bad luck," it's helpful to know it's all right to generate positive, productive thoughts and images as well. Who's going to stop you but yourself?

✄65✄

Psychic phenomena never solved a problem.
Neither did lotteries.

In spite of all I just said (in 64), you really do have to do the work to get it done. Visualizing winning the lotto won't help if you don't buy a ticket, and it won't help you solve dependency problems, mental weaknesses, depressions, even if you win. Psychic phenomenon is not abnormal or unhealthy. It's a part of the mind that's already there, a tricky part, but a part with a purpose. We can shut it down, but we can't destroy it, so we might as well learn the basics. Don't try to get what you haven't earned, don't try to see what isn't your business, don't try to force another person to think or act a certain way, don't get in other people's space, don't get revenge. These are not what this tool is for. The laws of ethics apply just as exactly to the psychic worlds.

The psychic mind is meant to be used for communication, survival, wisdom, visioning, problem-solving and creativity, especially when other methods aren't practical.

⮂66⮀

I once heard this in a dream:
the split between joy and discontent is 60/40.

When things are going bad and you are discontented, make an extra effort to be joyful. Don't take on unnecessary burdens, but look for ways to have fun, or better yet, have joy. Try to keep one step ahead of depression. Depression invades from behind and saps your strength without warning, so don't cut it too close. Have a little margin of extra happiness under your belt to cushion you. If things are going extraordinarily well, and life seems too soft, take on some challenges, extend help to those in need, spread your good fortune around. Trying to hoard all the smiles for yourself, trying for zero discontent doesn't work. It's like not paying your taxes, or not fixing your plumbing, and it leads to major unhappiness.

Depression is not discontent; good fortune is not joy. You decide to be discontented, just as you decide to be joyful. You can choose discontent even in the middle of splendor, if it keeps you striving for excellence. You can choose joy in the middle of squalor, if it keeps you on your toes. But the joy should edge out the competition by 60-40. "Accentuate the positive" is based on an old Greek idea that the world is slightly negative, so we need to balance it within ourselves.

Unhappiness is not always voluntary–good fortune is not necessarily voluntary either. But when these hit, we can always balance them out somehow and keep our life moving forward. That's my 1-step recovery program from uncontrolled happiness.

⮜67⮞

Be spontaneous—the devil can't hit a moving target.

Life is simple, but it's not graspable by the mind. Anyone who has a whole neat system of philosophy worked out is only looking at one side of the coin. There is a right side to everything that contradicts the left side of everything. There is a grandfather philosophy that can be worked out to perfection, and there is a grandmother philosophy that contradicts it.

In every field there are two schools of thought, and both have equally valid diplomas. The best you can do is graduate from one school before starting grade one of the other.

Any universe that hopes to contain the human race must be a perpetual motion machine, and that machine must have a clockwise spring and a counter-clockwise spring, a positive pole and a negative pole, a wave and a particle aspect, a decimal and fraction aspect, to stay moving. The male God and the female God can never be reconciled and won't be until the end of time. Soul stands at the end of time and reconciles them with a nod, but here in the physical world, there can never be a final answer, a final truce between opposites, or the world would stop spinning out new and infinite variations like a computer trying to compute Pi. Someone once said, "Women are from Venus, Men are from Mars." Remember that. It will never get boring.

Since there is no final word on anything, happiness depends on learning to suspend judgment, not clinging to finalities. Happiness involves being at one with the process, like a surfer on an endless wave. A surfer who is one with the process of surfing is spontaneous. No standing passively on the board wondering, "When will I hit the beachhead?" It's only when we look for finalities that we get stuck, and it's only when we get stuck that unhappiness sets in like the pedantic devil that it is and throws us into the drink. Stop blaming yourself for uncertainty, and start celebrating it—it won't disappear either way. One who celebrates uncertainty is certain to be spontaneous and will probably find a few happy coincidences that lead to rare truths along the way. Truths that are carved in stone are usually man-made. Smooth stones show the natural way.

SAYING

❧68❧

Don't try to say everything in one sentence.
You can never say it all.

(That just about says it all).

～69～

Getting one point across at a time is enough if done well.
One good sentence leads to another.

Speak organically, plant seeds in the mind of your listeners, and trust that they will grow into ideas, and the ideas into action. It is easier to smile and tread lightly when you have acorns in your pocket than when you are carrying a whole tree on your back.

If you do have to build an elaborate speech, try tracing the tree of your thoughts. Imagine you are a blind person describing a tree to other blind people. Start with the trunk, if you can find it, and touch it, putting your arms around it. Express what it is singly, in one sentence. Then gradually move up to the upper trunk, to see what the next sentence is. As limbs appear, choose one limb; when branches appear, choose one. When twigs appear, choose one, when leaves appear, choose only a sample few. This way, the ideas will flow from one another and show a truthful relationship.

If you need to say more, go back to the trunk again and start over. See where you end up. If the trunk is good, the branches will be good. If the branches are good, the leaves will be good.

Good speaking is knowing when to branch out and when to leave off.

❧70❧

Better to be silent than to speak with no purpose.

The great speakers, the great teachers, are open to silence, and from that small opening, great wisdom is given birth. If you claim the right to silence, you will be granted thunder. If you insist on the right to darkness, you will be able to hurl lightning bolts. When a wise teacher is thrown a deep question, he sinks deep below the surface to fish out the deep answer. If the querant isn't patient enough to wait for his thoughts to resurface, he is not ready for the answer. Sometimes, the answer may take a minute, a day, or a year. What's the difference? A glib answer is forgotten and floats away in a moment, but a deep answer stands like a marker for years of future travelers. And what if the answer doesn't come? Then the teacher becomes the student, and life becomes the teacher until the answer is found. That is the expansion of the known universe.

⮞70A⮜

Better to speak awkwardly
than to let a mistake go unreported.

As news journalists know, bad news is always hard for the compassionate to report, but it is also the most urgent and useful kind. Best to keep it simple. We need to be humble, and nothing humbles like humility.

Not only mistakes, but discoveries, revelations, and disagreements may need to be reported on a timely basis at the moment the cat has your tongue. Here, you are thrown between two possible complexities—that of forcing out a misworded and ill-advised statement that will never be forgotten, or of missing an opportunity to nip a problem in the bud. Make an "I" statement out of it. "I feel," "I have a theory that," "I heard that," rather than an accusing YOU statement, which is sure to cause anger. That's what I would do.

❧71❧

Speak as if no one would dare interrupt you.
If you can respect yourself this much, so will others.

The art of conversation in America is fading because there are too many interruptions and too little an attention span. It still takes more than thirty seconds to impart knowledge, but that's what the attention span of a hyperactive culture has whittled down to. It's time to build it up again, and that takes confident speakers.

Knowledge is information in context. Without knowledge, information is confused. Wisdom is experienced knowledge. Without wisdom, knowledge is shallow.

Good actors and public speakers fill themselves up with life, love, and light before going in front of the cameras. They feed themselves for the purpose of being a reservoir for others. The life, love, and light jump from the eyes like sparks and catch others by surprise. Rush ahead and you contradict this tone. When you rush, you reduce your words to information and not knowledge, and never wisdom. The good speaker never rushes but never loses sight of the goal.

The value of a word, musical note, fact, or idea comes from the context, the "relationship." Your insights into the "relationships" of things take a little more time to explain, but it's what's needed today. If you can't value yourself as one whom people will listen to, value what you have to say instead.

Loose talk devalues the currency of conversation. People interrupt devalued conversations just to state the obvious, but not valued ones. Avoid repeating yourself, using pointless speech, expressing vague opinions and generalizations. Speak with conviction and people will let you finish your point. When you are done, listen as attentively as you would like others to listen to you, and they may amaze you with their wisdom. Every person has a most fundamental need to express their sense of relationship with the universe, their identity, their thoughts, but the chance of hearing wisdom from another person's lips is perhaps the most precious opportunity.

⌇72⌇

*Speak directly, as if you know what you're talking about,
but humbly, as if you might be 90% wrong.*

The study of history reveals that 90% of what Thinkers thought a hundred years ago is wrong, or at least not entirely accurate. This being true, we have to wonder about ourselves today. There is a plague of narcissism going around that influences people to jump from one mental monkey bar to another, trying to save face, trying to look good. Truth becomes a lie—whatever will look good in print. But truth is not our invention. Natural truth comes from nature, and spiritual truth comes from spirit, but ignorance comes only from us. Remembering this, it is always easy to muster one's humility, even while convincing others that for all practical purposes you are right.

A person riddled with doubts will be ineffective as a communicator. Nothing is 100% certain, but for practical purposes you must speak as if it were, to avoid confusion. You need to have your thoughts and images clearly etched in your mind if you are to convey them directly into the mind of the listener. Unless you have made the mistake of putting yourself in an all-powerful position of absolute authority, you should have no problem correcting yourself. If, on the other hand, you've made that mistake, 'serves you right.

❧ 73 ❧

Uncertainty is as much a fact as anything else. Say only what you know is certain. If you're guessing, say so.

If you can say, "I don't know," with enough surprise and conviction, it makes people suspect that you must know something else by comparison.

Small-scale players seldom admit their ignorance because it overwhelms them. Big-scale players seldom admit their scope of knowledge because it overwhelms others and separates them from most of humanity. (It's lonely at the top, or so I've heard). Most of us, with practice, can enjoy the middle ground and can find enough certainties to keep up our end of the conversation, with plenty of mysteries yet to be solved. A good speaker can qualify each statement with "I don't know," "I guess," or "I'm certain that..." all of which is subject to the listener's fine tooth comb anyway.

With a scientist or journalist, the lines are as clear as fair and foul lines on a ball field, but in the realm of the seer, the psychic, the spiritual, one has to be especially careful to stay out of trouble. People who dabble in the psychic are most likely to bluff and hope when faced with things beyond their understanding. A true seer resists compulsive answers and waits for inner certainty, acting with grace rather than bluster.

A true seer works with forces mysterious to the average fellow and must be especially clear and deliberate when guessing, or even joking, or risk losing credibility later.

ঙ74ঙ

Don't believe everything you read. Go first hand, and suspend judgment about the rest. Withholding judgment builds up the muscles quicker than anything else.

The weak mind lets information slip by and muddles through it all, making excuses. The average mind clings to information, which closes the door to first hand knowledge and experience. The strong mind, however, can hold gently onto information and allow room for error and doubt, which encourages further exploration and discovery.

Reading and writing effect every part of our urban, money-driven lives, yet writing is nothing more than paper with lines, serifs, and curls stamped onto it. Like printed money, writing represents something powerful, but is not power itself. It is a currency of experience but is not experience. Some cultures do without writing or money quite happily. It is all what we make it.

Reading and writing is second best and is best second, which is to say that experience comes first so that books can re-enliven our memories of it afterwards. All our dreams, aspirations, fantasies, and imaginings are our own experience. Let the written word breathe life into such experiences, such dreams.

THE BODY

❧75❧

Nothing is stronger than a weakness.

Exercise each of your "bodies"; your physical one, your emotional one, your mental one, and your spiritual one; if you neglect any one of them, they may choose to go on strike; they'll just shut down, and you'll be spiritually out of service. These events aren't the work of the devil, they can be prevented. If you make each of the bodies strong, they will stand by you and do your bidding. If you allow them each to become weak, they will find other sources of energy and fight you at every step, because nothing is stronger than a weakness.

The forces of addiction, malignant narcissism, greed, sloth, vanity, etc., are energies that feed the weak and replace their powerlessness with a power that won't bend to a higher cause. This is how evil governments take over when the people feel powerless. The same thing can happen within you, and reversing such a trend may require revolutionary means. Preventative cures are the best kind. Take care of each part of your life, because a chain is only as strong as the weakest link, and stress seeks out the weakest link. Fast but don't starve the body, the heart, the mind, and the spirit. If you are going to dance, don't stand on only one leg. If you are going to clap, don't use only one hand; if you are going to sing, don't use just one note. Because if you don't use it, you lose it.

❧76❧

Unbearable pain is always in the past or the future, never in the present.

We build up our past pain by rehashing it, and we build up future pain with our fear. But the present is always bearable. "Be here now" is a blessing, not an admonishment. Future bliss turns to anxiety, past bliss turns to melancholy, but Now is the only moment when true bliss can occur.

I once was asked to help a friend, who was dying of cancer, deal with her pain. When I went to her bedside, this was the surprising pearl I found inside myself: "Unbearable pain is always in the past or future, never in the present." I shared it with her and she rejected it, saying, "You don't understand, it *is* unbearable!" I repeated myself, amazed at my own confidence in the inner teaching that had come through. She still argued. I didn't press it out of respect for her ordeal. Eventually, I had to leave, convinced that I had been unable to help her.

After she had passed away, her best friend confided to me that before passing, she left a message for me: she finally opened her heart to what I was saying and found it true, overcoming her pain in the final hours when she really needed to most. Her friend delivered a thank you from beyond the grave that has never been forgotten. I don't think she would mind my sharing it with you.

೫77೫

Breathing is living. If you're barely breathing,
you're nearly dead.

Breathing is a metaphor for life and is the most basic requirement of life. Breath is drawn into the blackness, breath goes out into the light. Life, too, comes and goes, from the dark and into the light, and back. When that dance ends, so ends our life as well.

Breath is the giver. It brings relaxation, and relaxation brings clarity and peace. Allow yourself to look at your own breathing as a picture of how your life is going. Do you breathe in a relaxed way? Are you allowing life to flow or are you fighting it? Breathing brings oxygen to the brain and all the organs, cleansing them so they can be helpful to you. Improve your breathing, and you may improve your life.

↜78↝

Your body is very wise, if you know how to listen.
Just because it's temporary doesn't mean it's disposable.

A healthy physical body registers and reacts to the activities of the emotional, mental, and spiritual "bodies." If you know what to listen for, you can learn a lot about yourself by reading your body's reactions. It doesn't lie...except when asleep.

When the healthy body feels frantic or numb, some part of you is in danger but doesn't know it yet. Artificial lights, irregular hours, the vibration of motors— all these throw off the body's balance and mask its signals, so make sure you keep listening carefully to the body, and take care of it. Animals know in their bodies when an earthquake or tornado is about to occur. They don't argue about it, they run.

People who are overly attached to the inner life try to sell it by saying that "the body is temporary, so why bother?" This is usually either said to counteract a fear of death or to deny responsibility for the real world.

Don't be fooled—the body may be temporary, but it is not disposable. You can't just get another one to replace it at the junk yard. Even if you leave it while dreaming, you have to wake up and smell the herb tea eventually.

You can't just throw junk down the hatch and pollute it right and left and expect it to kick on the next morning. The same people who have been running their bodies down in the name of hard work and the American dream are the ones who have been running the planet down. There is a profound connection between our body and the earth. Treat both with respect.

⸱79⸱

Bring strong emotions into your certainty,
not into your confusion.

Emotions have many purposes, and one is as a magnifier. They cause us to examine one aspect of our lives over and over again, until it becomes bigger than life. If you bring into your most lofty certainty the strength of emotions, you will be able to act on that certainty with undaunting courage. For most, certainties are fleeting and small and could use some magnifying. Uncertainties and confusion, however, are paralyzing and don't need to be magnified; they need to be seen clearly and soberly. Let your emotions run wild, and they will eventually leak into your uncertainty. Magnify uncertainty, and it will tear you apart.

∾80∾

For most people, self-improvement is simple:
turn off the TV!

Here's an interesting experiment. Keep a record of how much time you spend watching TV. If it's more than an hour any given day, consider spending that additional time relaxing and focusing, reading, exercising, or cleaning house instead. Most TV preempts self-improvement and does not have a calming effect, unless you are very upset about something. TV gives the illusion that something is happening in the room when it's not. If you're watching TV, (PBS not included) you're not busy, you're not relaxing, you're not thinking, you're not serving others, you're not improving, you're a couch potato growing green eyes. A majority of the truly interesting people I've interviewed as a journalist don't even own a TV.

However, I don't advocate the "blow up your TV" philosophy. I use the I Ching method of TV viewing, which is to wait for the right moment and then turn on the set, expecting to receive an important morsel of information. It usually works. If I can't find it within five minutes, I try to turn off the set, but you know how hard that is.

～81～

Believe in yourself, remember why you got into this line of work in the first place. Have integrity.

Integrity is an unimpaired state, a state of wholeness, full of honesty and sincerity. It means the different parts of you are integrated, and not running afoul of each other. In order to recover this wholeness state, it helps to go back to your earliest impulses towards creativity and goodness. What was the first step in the journey you are on right now? What were your good intentions, your aspirations? Analyze the mistakes you made, the decisions that weren't 100% effective along the way. Can you take responsibility for them and undo them, or compensate for them? Can you purify your life of their results? Can you start over at that same starting spot, and do better this time?

Starting your life over every morning is a wonderful way to begin each day, as refreshing as a dip in a lake. Take nothing for granted, but choose to be who you are every morning, and choose to do what you do, even if it's boring. If you have time, reinvent sliced toast before breakfast, reinvent the wheel before commuting to work. Create your world the way an artist creates a mood. Believe in yourself, and claim your right to change your life.

᧑82᧒

Live in this unique moment. Be in this particular place.
Only then will you make sense of the past
and foresee the future.

If you want to be strong enough to reach up to the stars, become grounded where you stand. You will know reality by its flaws, so take notice of imperfections—they alone are unique.

We are always imagining the future and reliving the past, trying to expand our sphere of power, thinking about anywhere but where we happen to be. Slow down the mind and see where you are. Slow down the mind some more and be where you are. Live in this small moment. As soon as you reach single-pointed beingness, you are everywhere.

The present contains the echoes of the past. See the present clearly and you can make sense of the past. Likewise, the present moment contains the rumblings of the future. See it clearly and you foresee the future. To see it clearly means to see its plainness, its smallness, its ordinariness. To see it clearly is to see the greatness where it might lead you. Greatness is in the details.

MONEY

❧83❧

It's enough just to be, and to love.
Everything else is gravy.

If you don't have love, nothing is enough. You will eat and eat and still be starving. If you are bursting with love, you are full even on an empty stomach, and everything else that comes to you is gravy.

If you choose love, no one can stop you from loving. If you choose to be, no one can stop you from being—even death can't erase the soul. Remember, you will always have enough if you choose to, and never enough if you choose not to.

When is it wise to choose just love? When you don't have a choice. When is it wise to ask for more? When the opportunity arises. Let your money-quest arise out of love and beingness, not fear and emptiness.We are living in a world based on nonbeing and nonloving pieces of silver, and it tends to rub off. Today, people fight over promotions and deals like fish fighting over a worm on a golden hook, and no one is the winner. Everyone who eats is in some way dependent on someone in that struggle, dad, mom, spouse, or government. You need to be responsible for your expenses, and pay your own way in some form. How do you balance all that? Perhaps one way is to remember that, while you're struggling, or supporting someone in the struggle, you're fighting over the issue of gravy, more versus less, gravy for yourself, or gravy for others, gravy today, or gravy tomorrow. It's a game you'll play better if you don't take it so personally. It's just gravy. A good experience is to live one year out in the woods on nothing. Many young people do this. They usually choose to come back and work and pay rent, but out of a desire to love and serve, not our of fear of poverty. The difference is like night and day.

❧84❧

Cast your fate to the wind, one shred at a time.

Life is an adventure, right? If not, why not? If you're like me, you don't want to miss any of the spectacle. You want to feel the power of the creative life stream coursing through your veins, taking you to new horizons, new mountain peaks of realization. Adventure implies danger, however, and so there are forces inside and out that hold us back from adventure, and from hidden traps we're not ready to see. Adventuring means stepping out into the unknown. One step is enough and leads to other steps. Jumping off a cliff however, only leads to one adventure that won't last very long, and it might be the last adventure you'll see for a long time. (Sometimes you *have* to jump, but that's another story. Look around for a parachute and just do it. As Yogi Berra once said, "When you come to a crossroads in life, take it!") As you explore the unknown, be prepared to solve problems as you go, and you can keep up a string of adventures longer than Joe DiMaggio's 56 game hitting streak.

❧85❧

Winning isn't everything,
but it does make a nice ending for your story.

Losing all the time is tedious and may indicate that you're not learning anything. Winning all the time...it's tedious and may indicate that you're not learning anything. Not that much difference! The heroes of legends usually took on big challenges, faced defeat, sometimes many defeats, and kept going. In the end they were victorious, but they were not two-dimensional characters. The stories we remember star three-dimensional characters who have their ups and downs and win in the end, even if only a moral victory. One of my favorite movies is "Tucker," a story about a real modern hero. He didn't go around kicking giants in the shins or stepping on ants. He tried to follow his own dream and when he came up against a huge wall, he tried to get around it. In the end, his victory was only one of principle, but it was heroic.

❧86❧

Consider each opportunity. If the heart says no,
go on to other opportunities.

People who follow their heart are usually go-getters, not slug-a-beds. Be eager for more advancement, but don't compromise your identity. Have faith that the universe will bring something suitable. Look back at your life and ask, how many times did I disobey my heart and regret it later? How many times was the heart wrong? In what areas was it wrong, and what areas was it right? Sometimes we have blind spots, but over all, our heart leads us into areas we need to learn about and can lead us out again. If the heart says no, and you proceed anyway, you're on your own. Then life gets complicated.

৵87৵

Let every relationship have nonprofit status:
Educational, religious, or for public service.

Most people desire a lot more from a relationship than a learning experience and a chance to serve others. But that's what makes sense out of most relationships.

Most of what you learn has to do with communication. You can learn plenty from a relationship without being able to communicate, but it's not ideal. Communication is relative; never totally present, and yet never absent. Silence speaks—talk is cheap. If a partnership forces you to learn to communicate in new ways, it's a precious learning experience. Let's say learning is Priority 1; the least, and perhaps the most, you should get out of a relationship.

Priority 2: Relationship as religious ordeal. If you put even the rockiest relationship in a spiritual perspective, you'll gain more from it. "What is God telling me through this dummy?" The pitfall of seeing the Divine in everyone is that the Divine is lying through some people's teeth, to get you to think for yourself.

Priority 3: Public service. Having a rough relationship is no excuse to drop the "I'm working for the good of the whole" attitude. Good results balance out bad. Whatever you can do for the good of the whole through the partnership is fair play, but you're still responsible for the relationship.

Of course, there are dozens of other things you want from a relationship, and at some point, if you've never gotten past the three basic priorities, you have to assess what you learned from the struggle and apply your principles towards a happier lifestyle. Success comes from finding harmonious relationships. Growth comes from handling difficult ones.

❧ 88 ❧

Mutual exploitation is not equality.

Mutual exploitation makes money (or power) the dominant partner. The dictionary says that exploitation may mean "to make use of," but also means "to make unethical use of for one's own advantage or profit. To make a profit from the labor of others." It's nice to be needed, but only if by expressed consent. Expression and consent are the key words. Two-way communication (expression) between two people in agreement (consent) must exist for there to be no exploitation. Exploitation is somewhat useful to society, but becoming useful through trickery, such as with plagiarism, strong-arming, and bait-and-switch, is not very satisfying because it does not involve consent. It is not allowing the second person free will and self-expression. Mutual exploitation is the short road to messy, complex, draining living. Mutual communication and support is the road to simpler, healthier, more vitalized living.

The old saying goes, "In Capitalism, man exploits his fellow man, but in Communism, it's just the other way around." Even champions of capitalist theory agree that the downfall of capitalism is exploitation, and I feel that mutual exploitation is only slightly better than one-way exploitation. (For more about the psychological roots of exploitation, read M.Scott Peck's, "The People of the Lie.")

↬89↫

In a simple world, those at the top take good care of those at the bottom.

Like the food chain we sit on top of, the higher levels depend on the more numerous lower levels to survive. The human depends on animals and plants and minerals, not the other way around. (They don't need us, except to get on PBS nature shows.)

Early humans knew there can't be more blocks at the top of a pyramid than at the bottom, but that is what's about to happen to our food chain as we overpopulate. In a simple economy, those at the top also take care of those at the bottom. But the administrators who are overpopulating have sucked the money to the top—no longer taking care of who or what is at the bottom, and the producers stop being productive. (If you want to find the supporting material for this statement, sift through "America: What Went Wrong?" a book by Donald L. Barlett and James B.Steel; Andrews and McMeel, Pub. Kansas City).

One of Nixon's economic advisors once told me, "Economics is an illusion," in hindsight, perhaps an embarrassing statement. Whether it's true or not, one thing is pretty solid—there is an underlying pyramid structure to the economic food chain. The earth itself, land, is the rock bottom basis of economy. Then there is the animal level, people (or animals) digging in mines, hauling things, growing (or becoming) food. This is still pretty close to the stable core of economics. Then come the salesmen, and other middlemen, who work on the emotional level, buying and selling. Their claim to the money is a little more tenuous, but the larger the society, the more we need these communicators. Then come the administrators, who coordinate complex work forces to try to insure efficiency and try to cover for the foibles of the salesmen. They are only as useful as their minds and live in a mental world of appearances. Then come the politicians who set the tone for the spirit of things, and who seem to change reality with a sweep of the hand. In the old days, the king was a proven hero, but today politicians are a little less than heroes: I would call them snake oil salesmen, but snake oil has been found to have some curative properties.

What all this leads to is this: if you want the fast money, you can join those at the top. If you want the slow money, work at the bottom. In an ideal world, that would be the richest road to follow, but not at the moment. Right now, everything is inverted. In other words, it's not easy making an honest dollar; there is no simple answer to economics. Perhaps the best thing is to not go for the short-run, or the long-run, but go for the slightly-long, not-too-short run. What would Buddha do with an MBA? He'd follow the middle path, and neither starve nor exploit others.

᭒90᭓

Make sure your support system is holding up something.

Make sure every bridge has a road on top. Make sure making a living has something to do with getting a life. Unlike bliss, administration without an object is worthless. Try to keep the good of the whole in mind in everything you do. Otherwise, your money won't talk any more—Rubles without a cause. Many are the times we have to back up and simplify, prune back the bushes, just so the flowers can get some sun.

Even if money doesn't rule your life, could your business be made yet simpler? Even if your scaffold does have a Michelangelo at the top, does it need repair?

The richest in spirit say, "Money is not what my life is about." Even in business relationships, money is never the only issue. How could it be any other way? How could you spend most of your day for most of your years doing something that has no meaning other than as a means to an end, knowing you could die at any moment? In America, fortunes are made and lost very quickly, and people who "make it" are then burdened with trying to keep it, a twenty-four hour a day job. Others who haven't made it yet see fortune just around the corner and can't let it out of their sight, even for a minute. Rare are those who are seeking their destiny rather than their fortune.

We are hooked on challenge, but if the challenge is a pointless one, we may end up as million-dollar a year flagpole-sitters, in pursuit of what's difficult without any reference to usefulness. If you're on the treadmill, one way to get off (without dropping everything) is to simplify your needs and use more of your support system to support people and causes you believe in, including yourself. Work towards your vision of a better life. If your friends live far away, spend the extra money on long distance telephone. Don't be a lonely miser. Take time for spiritual things, for your health, for sharing with nature, with people. Buy yourself a future, not just a present.

❧91❧

Financial wealth means freedom of choice only as long as you can choose to walk away from money.

People pray for Money to do what they want and always end up doing what Money wants instead. Money tells them to buy this house, that car, invest in that CD. Then it tells them when to pay the mortgage, the car payment, the insurance, the premium. Then the tax bills increase. Then it tells them that the line of work they love is not lucrative enough, and they'd better find a better paying line of work, or Money will be angry with them. When Money gets angry, look out! By then, it's too late to walk away from it. You owe it a blood sacrifice.

If you pray for Love, and do what it wants, you usually end up doing what you want as well. Love will tell you, don't buy this house, buy this one instead. It will always guide you away from pitfalls. If you continue working hard and loving what you do, you might find one day that you are rich. Love has sustained you and kept you free of greed even in the midst of Money. As one teacher once said to me, "Sometimes you have to do what you *don't* want to do before you can do what you *do* want to do." It takes a strong sense of where Love lies to go through a few years of that, but people have done it and so can you.

❧92❧

The best things in life are free, but never cheap.

Life will give us freely what we need to be happy and healthy, but then we have to take care of it with our own labors. We may find the puppy we desired on our doorstep, but it might grow up to be a Saint Bernard. Whenever there are three wishes, look out! Free means no down payment! It doesn't mean there won't be bills and expenses trickling in! Television is free and look where that has got us. Children are free, but ask the person who owns one if they're cheap. The snake gave Eve a free apple, and look what happened. On the other hand, the first commandment was free also, and Moses said, "I'll take ten!" God freely gave us the bounty of the earth, but we have to get down on our knees and plant good seeds once in a while too.

☙93☙

Don't borrow from more than one person,
or for more than one purpose.

This is another simple secret from the "simpler times of long ago." If you can manage the above, do it. At least it's more realistic for today's buyer than Poor Richard's "Neither a borrower nor a lender be." If he tried that today, he *would* be poor!

If you must borrow and borrow, just remember that in order to pay off a debt, you have to earn what you are already spending feverishly, plus 15% interest. The key to a simpler life is simple, "If you don't have it, don't spend it."

Of course, there are special exemptions for visionaries. Roy Disney once said to Walt, "You won't believe this. We're thirty million in debt!" Walt smiled and answered, "That's great. I remember when we were only three million in debt!" You have to give him credit (but not a line of credit), he was listening to the Love rather than the Money. If you love something so much you're willing to go to $30M in debt, you're in a special realm, somewhere past Nevernever Land.

THE FINAL ANSWER

ᕀ94ᕁ

*Don't try to tie everything together and nail it down.
It takes away all the fun.*

Reality is not a monster whose heart you must drive a silver stake of rationality through. Reality is a lot like you. It would like a little respect and some elbow room to move around. The universe is a living thing and can change its mind from time to time, so stop back seat driving. Experience and participation is the language of the Gods. Listen with your whole being to what your life is saying. The universe came up with you, so it must be pretty smart.

❧95❧

When hunting for truth, leave a hole in your net so you might hunt again tomorrow.

In the old Indian legends, the hunter Glooskap became such a great hunter that he hunted all the animals in the world and put them in his hunting sack. His wise old grandmother pointed this out to him and advised him to let most of the animals out so that there would be something to eat next year.

There is nothing wrong with hunting down the answers to life's questions, but be sure to leave your "bag" open-ended. If it's true that every individual appears on this planet for a purpose, to add something new to the mix, how could we living today possibly leave no hole unfilled? To create this illusion is to make barriers that future explorers will have to overcome. I like to compare truth-seeking with the Indian practice of tracking and tagging. You track down a wild animal and try to touch it without hurting it, and let it go. This way you learn a lot about animals. Today's zoologists tag animals in a different way, with a band, and then send them on their way—truth-seekers might practice the same kind of wisdom with pet theories...and pet facts too.

In this era when the origins of the universe are once again a mystery, we are reminded that we are in no danger of having all the answers. What a pleasant surprise!

❧96❧

Let life be a mystery. It will be grateful you did.

Some people make up world view "systems" and then close the book. They get stuck in their old realizations. Other people never have any realizations. Their world doesn't make sense to them, and so they, too, close the book on life, thinking the pages are blank. Both are far from experiencing the tantalizing mystery of the universe. Just as far away are religious people who say, "God is unknowable and unknown," or "My church has all the answers, and I'm saved anyway so don't bother me with facts."

Everything that moves is inter-related, and interdependent, but those connections are hidden to the naked eye. You could spend your whole life walking from one spiritual connection to the other like stepping stones across an endless river of questions and never get to the end, and then you would know how it is that the unfathomable mystery makes so much sense.

❧97❧

Follow your bliss, you never know where you'll end up.

It's never too late to start looking for bliss. We are like blades of grass underneath a stone. We seek the light or die trying. We try bending this way, then that way, until we eventually are touched by a ray of sunshine. We are soft and flexible, and very simple in nature, just like the lowly grasses; yet by constant perseverance, we can split a concrete slab in two.

❧98❧

Theories about life are fine, but if you can't dance to it,
it ain't music.

You can predict the course of planets, but not people. Ecstatic and impulsive behavior distinguishes us from rocks, computers, and tax collectors. When the divine, creative spark enters, there's no telling what will happen. Each interaction with the divine brings an element of surprise, even humor. When we break out of our little self-constructed boxes, we find the missing pieces of the puzzle, the moment of "aha" that moves us forward. The divine is not just in our minds, it's in everything else as well. When the wind from the mind meets the wind from the divine, these two fronts can create a storm, a flash flood, thunder and lightning, and these dramatic side-effects let you know: Reality is taking place, and it's beyond your control.

Surprise is a dead giveaway that you are not alone in the universe. It's what makes birthdays fun, jokes funny, love loving, and life worth living.

If you've "gotten with the program" and you're still not sure why there's a program, maybe you need to face up to some soft realities. Maybe your primary responsibility is to enjoy the dance of life more, to dip into the unpredictable, and take a few risks so that you keep growing.

There's something to the expression, "Love, serve, and remember." We remember the surprise of the divine, and so we start loving and serving. Soon we start organizing, planning our means of serving, until every day is booked solid with loving and serving chores. Somehow we've ceased to remember what we are loving and serving. If you get to this intersection, don't turn left or right, back up and find the fun in what you're doing.

✌99✌

Do the right thing. You'll feel better.

Philosophers spend hours debating what right and wrong are, but if you do something that's difficult, painful, beneficial, and you feel better afterwards, that was the right thing to do. If you do something that's easy, pleasurable, and inane, and other people feel better afterwards, that was the right thing too.

It's only through trial and error that we find out which things will make us (and others) feel better after we do them, and which will make us feel worse. Of course, this isn't a hard and fast ontological, theological, existential, orthopedic rule. Ultimately, you have to decide for yourself what's right and wrong—without landing in jail.

❧100❧

Where possible, finish A before going on to Z.

Try to at least browse through a few of the pages before peeking at the end to see how it turns out. If you are learning yoga, don't try the grand lotus position, or the headstand, until you have at least learned to breathe. Don't swim the English Channel until you can at least stand up in the bath tub. Don't play the eighteenth hole before you've finished the second. Don't announce you are God before learning to control your temper. And where possible, finish A before going on to Z, you'll enjoy life more.

Evan T. Pritchard is best known for his writing in Resonance Magazine, of which he is founder and editor. Like many publishers, the scope of his interests suggest the term "Renaissance Man"—one step away from "philosopher," and about as useful. He has made his living as a classical guitarist, singer, symphonic composer, painter, legal assistant, copyright clerk, song-writer, stand-up comic, cartoonist, househusband, publisher, poet, editor, reviewer, journalist, school teacher, word processor/secretary, construction worker, agent, producer, enterpreneur, bookstore owner, radio personality, consultant, and world traveler. He is the author and co-author of a number of books. He has interviewed more than fifty outstanding inspirational artists and has worked closely with a number of Native American Medicine Men, lamas, and masters. He is a father of a six-year-old boy (David, to whom this book is dedicated) and is currently painting his picket fence.